■ EDITED BY LITA LINZER SCHWARTZ

PSYCHOLOGY AND THE MEDIA: A SECOND LOOK

American Psychological Association
Washington, DC

Published by
American Psychological Association
750 First Street, NE
Washington, DC 20002

Copies may be ordered from
APA Order Department
P.O. Box 92984
Washington, DC 20090-2984

In the U.K., Europe, Africa, and the Middle East, copies may be ordered from
American Psychological Association
3 Henrietta Street
Covent Garden, London
WC2E 8LU England

Typeset in Palatino by EPS Group Inc., Easton, MD

Printer: AGS, White Plains, MD
Cover Designer: Design Concepts, San Diego, CA
Technical/production editor: Jennifer Powers

Library of Congress Cataloging-in-Publication Data
Psychology and the media : a second look / edited by Lita Linzer
    Schwartz.
        p.   cm.—(Psychology and the media ; 2)
    Includes bibliographical references and index.
    ISBN 1-55798-578-2 (pbk.: alk. paper)
    1. Mass media—Psychological aspects.   I. Schwartz, Lita
Linzer.   II. Series.
P96.P75P86   2000
302.23'01'9—dc21   99-34543
                                                            CIP

British Library Cataloguing-in-Publication Data
A CIP record is available from the British Library.

Printed in the United States of America
First Edition

Contents

Contributors

Rochelle Balter, PhD, is in private practice in New York. She is a cognitive–behavioral therapist and is coauthor of *Overcoming Performance Anxiety*. She is coordinator of Psychologists with Disabilities, an advocacy group concerned with psychological issues and physical disability. Her research interests include the social psychology of disability, especially how those with physical disabilities are portrayed by the media.

Michael S. Broder, PhD, is a psychologist, author, popular speaker, radio host, and leader of continuing education workshops for professionals. He was the first president of Division 46 (Media Psychology), has hosted radio programs for all three major networks as well as locally in New York and Philadelphia, and has appeared on hundreds of national and local radio and television programs. His work has been featured in numerous professional publications and in *Newsweek, USA Today, TV Guide*, the *New York Times*, the *LA Times*, the *Chicago Tribune*, the *Wall Street Journal*, and the *Washington Post*. Broder practices in Philadelphia, where he also oversees the psychological services for the Philadelphia Police Department. He is the founder of Media Psychology Associates, which consults to a wide variety of professional, business, health care, employee assistance, education, and law enforcement organizations.

Rhea K. Farberman is the associate executive director for public communications at the American Psychological Association (APA). In her position, she directs the APA's media relations program and is the executive editor of the APA's newspaper, the *Monitor*. An accredited member of the Public Relations Society of America (PRSA), Farberman serves on the board of directors of PRSA's Healthcare Academy. She is an honors graduate of American University's School of Communications and completed graduate studies in public relations management at George Washington University.

Dan Gottlieb, PhD, a practicing psychologist for 30 years, is a past president of the Family Institute of Philadelphia and a clinical assistant professor at Allegheny and Widener Universities. He has directed substance abuse programs in Philadelphia and was appointed by Department of Health and Human Services Secretary Donna Shalala to the National Advisory Board of the Center for Mental Health Service in 1987. In recognition of his professional work; service as host of the "Voices in the Family" program on WHYY radio, Philadelphia; and his semimonthly columns in the *Philadelphia Inquirer,* Gottlieb has received awards from the American Association of Marital and Family Therapists, the Pennsylvania Psychological Association, and the New Jersey Family Therapy Association.

Phyllis R. Koch-Sheras, PhD, is in private practice in Charlottesville, VA, and is an adjunct assistant professor at the University of Virginia. She is the founder and president of the Creative and Healing Arts Institute and a former president of the Virginia Applied Psychology Academy. She specializes in work with groups, couples, and dreams, and is the author of books and articles on dreams and relationships. She also has experience in radio and television and as an opera singer.

Rosalie Greenfield Matzkin, EdD, teaches mass communications and media arts courses at Pennsylvania State University's Abington College. Aside from her current and previously published work in the area of media effects and youth, she has been researching, writing, and lecturing on film audiences, the portrayal of women in film, and the American musical theater. Before getting her doctorate from Teachers College at Columbia University, she spent 6 years working in the mass media as a trade newspaper reporter and editor and in local news television as a political researcher in New York. She also spent 2 years in New York doing public relations.

Patricia Pitta, PhD, ABPP, is a family psychologist in private practice in Manhasset, NY. She holds a diplomate from the American Board of Family Psychology and is an adjunct clinical professor at St. John's University, Queens, NY. Pitta has published many articles on the integration of family and psychodynamic theory applied to children, adolescent, marital, and individual treatment. She is an active member of the APA and has held many offices throughout the years. She is presently the secretary of Division 46 and a member-at-large of Division 42. She was honored as the "Family Therapist of the Year" by the Long Island (NY) Association of Marriage and Family Therapy in 1998. She is also an approved supervisor of the American Association of Marriage and Family Therapy.

Lita Linzer Schwartz, PhD, ABPP (Forensic), is a Distinguished Professor Emerita at the Pennsylvania State University. Her teaching at Penn State's Abington College has been focused on psychology and education, as well as forensic psychology. Her media contacts on behalf of the university as well as her writing emphasize areas that affect children and youth: divorce and child custody, giftedness and creativity, cults, and families by adoption. Committed to interdisciplinary research, she is currently working on a book on neonaticide and infanticide with a historian colleague (also allegedly retired) and on an expansion of her chapter with Rosalie Greenfield Matzkin.

Peter L. Sheras, PhD, is associate professor in the Curry Programs in Clinical and School Psychology at the University of Virginia in Charlottesville. He is the past director of the Center for Clinical Psychology Services and a former president of the Virginia Psychological Association. He specializes in work with adolescents, families, and couples and appears frequently on radio and television and in print about couples and teenagers. He has experience as a video producer and a child actor. He is an author of books and articles on clinical psychology, dreams, youth violence, parenting stress, and relationships.

Foreword

It is with great pleasure that Volume 2 in our book series on Psychology and the Media is presented under the auspices of Division 46 (Media Psychology) and the American Psychological Association. This book should serve as an excellent companion to Volume 1, *Perspectives on Psychology and the Media* (Kirschner & Kirschner, 1997). Read separately or in combination, the volumes highlight the major dilemmas and delights that beset and beckon those who enter into the various domains in which psychologists and the media interact. Whether we give or host interviews on air, on camera, on film, or in newspapers or magazines, we are trying to enhance the mental health of individuals, couples, families, and communities. We try to inject optimism within the context of realistic appraisals of situations. We seek to provide accurate information based on the most up-to-date research and clinical findings and reports.

Sometimes our goals conflict with those of the media, which may seek to sensationalize a story, to tell the most gruesome details, to portray violent and sexual material, or to provide sound bites or brief, condensed print columns. When this occurs, we can try to educate or otherwise influence media personnel, although this may not be acceptable to them, or we can decline to participate in programs, coverage of news stories, or as consultants to films or videotapes we believe are detrimental to the viewer, inaccurate, or unethical.

In this volume, the authors discuss a smorgasbord of fascinating topics. Editor Lita Linzer Schwartz has succeeded in bringing together a bevy of experts, each of whom enlightens us on their topic in a highly readable style. We commend the authors and the editor for bringing us this finely honed volume and believe most psychologists and other mental health professionals will find it worth reading and keeping nearby as an instructive reference.

Florence W. Kaslow

Reference

Kirschner, D. A., & Kirschner, S. (1997). *Perspectives on psychology and the media.* Washington, DC: American Psychological Association.

Preface

A book is one medium for communicating ideas, although not on the grand scale of the mass media with which this volume is concerned. As a person and as a media psychologist, I welcome the opportunity to read material that communicates effectively. I believe that the contributors to this volume have achieved this. Writing styles of the authors and modes of presentation differ, but each chapter not only provides information and guidance that may be new and helpful but also offers insights into the ways in which each author thinks about the role of the media psychologist in today's world.

What the contributors will tell you—you, the psychologist who is interacting with the media—is to think carefully about *what* you are trying to communicate, *who* you are trying to communicate with, and *how* you and your content are likely to be perceived and to do so in a somewhat different manner than you do when interacting with professional colleagues. As important as these three elements are in reporting (i.e., *what*, *who*, and *how*), the other three elements, the *when*, *why*, and *where*, also are critical to being an effective media psychologist. The *when* and *where* provide the context for the content to be provided, and the *why* may determine the length of the response and the level of language used in the response.

Being a media psychologist can be an exciting challenge, a vital new experience, or a source of frustration—or perhaps all three at once. If it is primarily a new experience, the practical guidance in this book will prove invaluable. If you already work with some forms of media, but not others, you may be encouraged to branch into new areas after reading this book. As each of the authors in this volume stress, as a media psychologist, it is important to keep in mind that when you interact with the media, you not only speak for yourself but also represent your profession. I hope that this book helps you to communicate caringly and with care!

As editor of the volume, I owe particular thanks to Florence W. Kaslow, Publications Chair of the Division of Media Psychology (Division 46) of the American Psychological Association (APA), for encouraging me to participate in this exciting venture. Julia Frank-McNeil, Director of APA Books, was supportive and helpful in many, many ways and always responded to my queries promptly, as did Margaret Schlegel, development editor for the volume. Finally, it was a pleasure to work with colleagues who were committed to the task they had undertaken. Every one of the authors was cooperative and remarkably tolerant when I asked them for something more. I extend my thanks to each of them.

Introduction

Lita Linzer Schwartz

Although research is certainly involved in almost all publications and presentations by psychologists, some of it is basic research, and some of it is applied. In this second volume sponsored by Division 46 (Media Psychology) of the American Psychological Association (APA), the emphasis is on the latter. Several chapters include descriptions of practical aspects of interacting with the media: opportunities, challenges, difficulties, and recommendations. In dealing with the media, our focus often tends to be almost exclusively on television programming, which pervades (and often invades) our lives 24 hours a day. Here, we include other types of media as well, such as radio, newsprint, computers, and films, to offer a more rounded view.

When we think of television pervading and invading our lives, however, images of the Gulf War and, more recently, Kosovo, the O. J. Simpson criminal trial, the Oklahoma City bombing and subsequent trial, Princess Diana's death, shootings at schools, and other events immediately come to mind. Certainly, the APA and the ongoing National Television Violence Study, as well as the efforts of other groups and individuals, have focused more attention on violence in television programming in the past few years than was true heretofore. President Clinton, in his State of the Union address in January 1997 and in his commencement address at San Diego State University in June 1997, drew attention to racism in our society and the need to combat it. Ted Koppel, on his *Nightline* telecast (ABC-TV) of May 6, 1998, discussed the presence (or absence) of several racial and cultural groups on television—notably, the almost total absence of Asians and Native Americans and disproportionately few Hispanics (except perhaps in the Miami area). [Note: Among the programs introduced in the 1998–1999 season were at least two

1

sitcoms featuring Black families. Neither was reviewed too favorably; Leonard, 1998.] The media, again especially television, have contributed to these problems of violence and racism in both sitcoms and other programming. Talk radio and the press, however, also are strong influences on our perceptions of violence and racial issues.

Other media presentations that influence popular perceptions of people and contemporary life include changing views of working women, the family, sports and entertainment figures, the physically challenged, and other groups. These may also be found in the print media, including the full spectrum of magazines, as well as radio, television, films, and now the Internet.

The Public Broadcasting System, some cable channels, public-service broadcasts, magazines, newspapers, and web sites make information readily available in this country and around the world. The media use psychologists to provide insights, counsel, and an informed perspective through newspaper and magazine columns, radio broadcasts, and television appearances. Others are "on call" as sources of information for the media when a disaster occurs or when psychologically relevant questions need answering. Some psychologists present college-level courses and supervision using distance learning via television, whereas others advise network producers on sensitive issues, particularly for public broadcasting.

It is very difficult to comment on one aspect of the media without considering its ramifications and its effects on other media presentations and on the viewers or listeners. In short, the ripple effect of the media can be endless, especially with the long-term storage capacities of computer technology now available. That being the case, we as psychologists need to study not only the present effects of our interaction with the media and the effects of the media on us and others but also how our interactions may be interpreted in the future.

Although media psychology is a relatively new discipline, there are long-term perspectives that are relevant to this volume. For example, radio has been our companion and a vital part of our lives for about three fourths of the century, and television for just over half a century. A recent article in the *Journal of Social Issues* (Pandora, 1998) focused on the role of radio as seen in the mid-1930s by Hadley Cantril and Gordon Allport, as well as many other psychologists. During World War II, for example, Edward R. Murrow's broadcasts from London in the Blitz had as great an impact on audiences as CNN's telecasts of the Gulf War did half a century later. Television has made us visual as well as auditory witnesses to sensitive controversies, such as the events surrounding the impeachment of President Clinton. The way television presents the issues can heavily influence our perceptions and evaluations of the issues involved. As former president of the Division of Media Psychology Marion Gindes (1998) has observed, psychologists today are in an important position to help both the public and media representatives sift through these issues in a responsible way.

Except for Volume 1 of this series, *Perspectives on Psychology and the Media* (Kirschner & Kirschner, 1997), there is no other literature that specifically pulls together the multifaceted fields of psychology, media, and communications. Because so many psychologists wish to become more informed about working with the media, this book is a much needed addition to the literature that will both stimulate professionals' thinking and guide them in ethical practices.

The book is divided into two parts: One speaks to interacting with the media, and the other focuses on the treatment of specific topics by the media. Occasionally, a colleague in one part writes something that dovetails beautifully with something a colleague in the other part has written. This is the case, for example, with Dan Gottlieb's comments about how he dealt with his physical disability publicly on his radio program and Rochelle Balter's chapter dealing with how the media has portrayed the physically challenged. These complementary perspectives make for a much richer understanding of a previously neglected topic in media psychology.

It is important to remember that for psychologists, "the media are the messengers to share our expertise and knowledge with the public" (Warren & Friedland, 1996, p. 1). This book is offered with the hope that more psychologists will build effective relationships with the media that can help improve the quality of life for us all.

References

Gindes, M. (1998, Fall). From the president's desk. *Amplifier* [Division 46 newsletter], 1.

Kirschner, D. A., & Kirschner, S. (Eds.) (1997). *Perspectives on psychology and the media.* Washington, DC: American Psychological Association.

Koppel, T. (1998, May 6). *Nightline.* New York: American Broacasting Company.

Leonard, J. (1998, September 14). Black flight: Two new sitcoms feature Black families in the cushy suburbs, but only one rings true. *Time,* 80.

Pandora, K. (1998). "Mapping the new mental world created by radio": Media messages, cultural politics, and Cantril and Allport's *The Psychology of Radio. Journal of Social Issues, 54,* 7–27.

Warren, J., & Friedland, L. (1996, Spring). The media are the messengers. *Amplifier* [Division 46 newsletter], 1.

I

Shaping Media Portrayals Through Interaction: Print, Radio, and TV

Whenever a major event occurs, particularly a negative one, the media seek professional input to help explain the effects of violence or of some traumatic manmade or natural event. The American Psychological Association (APA) and its members become important sources of information to the media as well as of professional assistance to victims. In Chapter 1, Rhea K. Farberman of the APA Public Information Office provides clues not only to the ways in which we can help the media but also how to get word to the media of matters that are important to psychologists. This is more than honing our public image; it is educating the public. She also is educating us.

Farberman and others in this section touch on the question of "on-air therapy" via radio or the high-profile television programs that tend to focus on sensitive or embarrassing personal matters. Michael S. Broder, a practitioner, shares his experiences with radio and other media in a decidedly non-pedantic fashion. Dan Gottlieb, who hosts a program on the PBS station in Philadelphia and writes a column for the *Philadelphia Inquirer*, shares his thoughts on interacting with people via voice and print, with some comments on the differences between the two. He also brings to his work the voice of the physically challenged, which is an important element in the rapport he establishes with his audience. None of these practitioners assume the "know-it-all" or highly prescriptive expert role of some radio or television personalities, nor do they exploit the pain of their clients.

There are other aspects of psychologists' interaction with the media. Peter L. Sheras and Phyllis R. Koch-Sheras tell of how they use the many types of media to promote positive images of couples, their primary area of focus. In a sense, they enlarge on Farberman's chapter and incorporate much of what other media practitioners have expressed here, albeit with a unique perspective.

All of these chapters discuss psychologists' interactions with the media—the positive aspects as well as the pitfalls. Although they are not all meant to be prescriptive, they should alert the reader to some of the media practices about which any psychologist should be aware as well as to provoke ideas that may stimulate the reader to become a better prepared "interactor" with the media.

A cautionary note might be added here with respect to litigation and professional liability. Whether a psychologist has a printed column, hosts a radio or television program, is a guest on someone else's program, or is asked to provide specific therapeutic advice via telecommunications (e.g., Internet, electronic mail, or telephone), the psychologist must be extremely careful. It would be extremely unethical to provide such specific advice for an unknown "client," could conceivably violate rules of confidentiality even with a known client, and would make the professional vulnerable to a lawsuit in the event of a negative or undesired outcome. Recommending that the person see a professional, or meet with a support group or ask himself or herself some thoughtful questions about a troubling situation is not as perilous as offering the psychological equivalent of "Take two aspirin and call me in the morning."

Chapter 1

What the Media Need From News Sources

Rhea K. Farberman

According to the newsletter *Public Relations Tactics* (Public Relations Society of America, 1996), health information is what news editors and producers want most from public relations professionals and other news sources. Indeed, health news and medical research are among the most widely (and some would say poorly) reported news worldwide.

For psychologists and behavioral researchers, the media reporting of news and current events offers a credible, far-reaching, and inexpensive way to educate large numbers of Americans about psychological findings and knowledge. For the news media, psychologists are interview sources who can help answer the "why" of news events and social trends and can add interest, credibility, and a fresh or unique angle to the news. So why is the relationship such a tenuous one?

When Journalism Meets Psychology

When journalism and psychology meet, two very different worlds are coming together. The foundation of psychology is the careful analysis of research done over time. The foundation of journalism is the clock, or too often the stopwatch;

a continuous rush to meet deadlines and beat the competition.

Understanding what is considered news by the gatekeepers of the news process (reporters, editors, and producers) is a key factor in successful media relations. What is important to realize is that many of the decisions made during the process by which an event becomes news are subjective. Whereas most editors and producers will tell you that they make decisions about what gets in the paper or on the air based on objective factors such as timeliness, uniqueness, significance, impact on the community, proximity to the audience, drama, and the availability of good visuals, that person's view of the world also enters into the decision-making process.

The American Psychological Association Public Affairs Office

The American Psychological Association (APA) Public Affairs Office and its counterpart in the Practice Directorate work on a daily basis not only to make the news media aware of the knowledge and expertise of psychologists but also to prepare psychologists to be successful newsmakers. APA's media referral service is an electronic database that records the area of expertise and media experience of approximately 1,500 APA members who have expressed an interest in doing media work. The system works as a matchmaker, putting the journalist in touch with the right psychologist, one who can answer questions intelligently and in a speedy fashion. This service lists psychologists with expertise in approximately 150 subject areas, from child development to intelligence tests, from eating behavior to sports psychology. In an average year, between 5,000 and 6,000 APA members are referred to journalists for interviews through the referral service.

Interpreting and publicizing the research published in APA journals is another way the organization seeks to educate the media, and through them the public, about the value and contributions of psychology and psychological research. APA

Public Affairs staff review all journal articles and books published by APA for news potential and write press releases based on those judged most likely to attract the interest of editors, reporters, and producers. Between 35 and 40 press releases based on APA journal articles and books are distributed to the media each year.

During the mid-1990s, APA made a large investment in educating the public about the value of psychological services and undertook similar but smaller projects to inform the public about the importance of behavioral research. These investments however, while unprecedented in the over-100-year history of the organization, are dwarfed by the investments other organizations and corporate America make in communicating with the public. For example, the APA public education campaign was funded at the level of $1 million dollars a year for 5 years. When Lays wanted to introduce its fat-free potato chip to American consumers, it spent over $40 million dollars in a 6-month period on advertising and marketing!

The costs of communicating directly to the public through paid advertising make news media relations all the more important for psychology. It is important to remember that those professions and organizations that build ongoing relationships with the news media have a voice when important news breaks and when national policies are discussed. Those organizations that remain silent or are not proactive in their communications efforts will be stuck on the sidelines of most news events and public policy debates. The American Medical Association and the American Psychiatric Association are two examples of vocal participants in news media reporting of current events and active players in the Washington public policy arena.

"If you want your views represented, you have to talk to the media," said Roger Allies, a former media adviser to George Bush (cited in Sherman, 1989, p. 73). The problem with not talking to the news media is that reporters will find other sources to talk to, explained Allies. Those sources may not understand an issue as well as you do and probably will not cast you and your research, university, profession, as you would.

Nearly 20 years ago, TV news elder statesman David Brinkley noted that when a government or industry spokesperson "deals with television, it is not us they are dealing with. They are dealing with the American people through us. They give clear, short answers because they are more effective when they are delivered by us to the American people" (cited in Rafe & Pfister, 1983, p. 56). The news media's ability to be the conduit through which organizations speak to the American public is larger and even more powerful today. A 1996 Harris Poll found that Americans' most important source of news, by a 2 to 1 margin, was Cable News Network (Kalish, 1996). And, for the limited number of Americans who get their news from other sources, television news still sets the standard for how news and information are reported.

Most psychologists agree that it is important for organized psychology to build and maintain ongoing relationships with the news media. But most would also agree that media relations can be a double-edged sword. If you don't know what you're doing, you can get hurt.

Special Opportunities and Special Problems

As the news media offers opportunities for psychology and psychologists, it also presents special problems, including (a) the uninformed reporter, (b) fitting complex research into a sound bite, (c) patient confidentiality, and (d) public education versus "on-air" therapy.

The Uninformed Reporter

Typically, the reporter assigned to do a story with psychological implications has a limited understanding of psychology and behavioral science. The exception would be a large media outlet with the resources to assign an experienced writer to the psychology beat. Only a few national outlets, such as the *New York Times*, have such a reporter. What is more likely is that the reporter who calls the psychologist for comment or explanation of a new piece of research or a news event is a generalist, called a *general assignment reporter* in the industry.

An investment of time and patience is required when dealing with the inexperienced reporter, but that investment is critical to the quality and accuracy of the final story. A good piece of advice to the news source—the interviewee—one should approach the reporter as one would approach a student. Think of the interview as a teaching opportunity, and as such, communicate to the student (the reporter) in language he or she can understand.

The Foundation for American Communications (1990) *Media Resource Guide* has the following to say about the importance of providing background material to reporters:

> The key to background information is the knowledge that the craft of news reporting is very much a story-to-story, day-to-day profession. Unless you are blessed with a reporter covering you regularly, odds are that any reporter covering a story involving you may not know very much about you, the story, and what happened before the reporter was assigned to your story. The protection you need in that situation also happens to be an effective way of providing service to the reporter. Who knows more about you than you do? By compiling basic information, you can make the reporter's job easier. (p. 13)

In other words, by taking the time to educate the reporter and provide him or her with all appropriate background material, you are making an investment in more thorough, more accurate news coverage.

Fitting Complex Research Into a Sound Bite

The average news sound bite today is under 10 seconds in length. But psychological research is complex, and there are limitations as to how resulting data should be interpreted and applied. Caveats are important. Simply put, what the researcher sees in his or her research results—one piece of the overall research puzzle that can be applied only within the limits of this particular study—is different from what the reporter wants to find in a research study—the all encompassing headline.

The challenge for the news source, the psychologist, is how to translate the research into a meaningful sound bite; this is especially true when preparing for interviews with electronic media (i.e., radio and television), which often emphasize speed and brevity above in-depth reporting.

One valuable strategy for doing so is for the researcher to ask himself or herself simple questions about the research study. What was the goal of the research? What theory did I set out to prove or disprove? How might the results of this study be applied in the future? Brief but descriptive answers to these questions create a sound bite that is simple without being simplistic. Also consider the media outlet you are being interviewed by. The type of interview you would do with your community newspaper is different from the one you would do with National Public Radio and different again from the one you would do with a network evening magazine like ABC's *20/20*.

Patient Confidentiality

Reporters are looking to personalize the news and to make it dramatic. Often with issues in clinical psychology, reporters or news producers will ask psychologists to provide names of patients whom the reporter can also interview or who can appear on a broadcast with the mental health provider. These requests create vexing dilemmas for psychologists. Some, indeed many, psychologists feel that their responsibility to uphold patient confidentiality would rule out giving reporters the names of patients, either current or past. Other psychologists see the value, in terms of helping other people with similar issues who are not yet in therapy, of giving the media the opportunity to humanize and personalize the ailment by allowing them to introduce a person who is struggling with it or has conquered it. The Division of Media Psychology and APA's Public Information Committee have looked at this issue in depth and have found both value and areas of concern. The Division's suggestions for psychologists working with the news media are as follows:

> When considering using clients on air, psychologists weigh several issues carefully, and where the needs of the psychologist and patient differ, the patient's welfare always comes first. Among the factors to be considered are: the vulnerability of the patient; whether or not the appearance of the patient would be exploitative; whether the patient is deciding to participate to please the therapist; and whether the appearance is a perceived testimonial or a demonstration of a therapeutic technique. The public education value of the appearance should also be considered. (American Psychological Association, Public Information Committee, 1996, p. 33)

Public Education Versus On-Air Therapy

Experienced media psychologists all recognize that educating the public about psychology and psychological interventions is not therapy nor should it be. The value of media psychology is to inform consumers about how psychology could help them or their loved ones. At its best, media psychology can suggest alternative behaviors and can motivate people to look at a situation with a new perspective or to seek the assistance of a mental health professional for a problem. Media psychology cannot, however, in and of itself, solve the complex problems that are part of many people's lives today.

It was precisely the limits of what media psychology can and should do that caused so much disquiet within the profession about the talk show phenomenon of the early to middle 1990s. At that time, talk shows were increasing in number, each trying to outdo the other in terms of the startling personnel or outrageous on-air behavior. The shows were numerous, *Jenny Jones, Ricki Lake,* and *Montel Williams,* to name a few. Each wanted mental health professionals to "perform" as part of the show's formula: conflict for the first 50 minutes and then a resolution by a therapist during the last 2 broadcast minutes. Although the shows were successful in being able to attract "therapists" to appear on air, many experienced media psychologists refused to take part.

Why Do the News Media Do the Things They Do?

What drives the news media? Time, the quest for accuracy and fairness, and competition with other outlets—but mostly time. The only way to really appreciate the time pressures under which journalists work, particularly reporters who work in radio, television, and on daily newspapers, is to be aware of them.

Reporters writing for daily newspapers typically receive a story assignment in the morning and face a deadline that afternoon. In this time, the reporter has to quickly educate him- or herself about the issue, ascertain the facts, and get quotes from people involved or other knowledgeable experts, to achieve balance between both sides of a story. All this has to be done in anywhere from 4 to 6 hours. Often, the news source who returns the reporter's call most promptly or who is most helpful to the reporter's understanding of the issues involved is the person who gets quoted or has the most effect on the story.

Radio journalists face even tighter deadlines, as radio tries to provide listeners with something that newspapers cannot: hourly updates on the news. Often a radio station will want to do a news interview with a source immediately, or certainly that same day.

Television deadlines range somewhere between the immediate need of radio and the "this afternoon" deadlines of print reporters. But TV has an added dimension. Whereas the majority of interviews for print and radio journalists are done over the phone, television reporters want to go to the news source's office or to some other appropriate setting to do the interview (and get "pictures" to go along with the story). The TV reporter has to leave the studio and get video tape; that adds time and pressure to the news-gathering process.

Deadlines vary in television. Daily morning or afternoon broadcasts want to do interviews the same day, or at times do live interviews during the actual broadcast. Other types of television news, like weekly magazine format shows, have longer lead times and typically work on a show segment 4 to 6 weeks in advance of its airing.

The need for speed does not always allow the media to find the best fit between news source and story. It also doesn't always allow the reporter time to do the necessary homework to get grounded in a topic area before conducting an interview. Such situations put both the news outlet and the news source at risk of a story or a quote that is incorrect or out of context or incomplete. The news organization cannot do much to change the nature of the news-gathering process and the news cycle. They certainly cannot add hours to the day. News sources can, however, take a few steps to try to be as efficient and effective as possible in spite of the media's time pressures.

How to Level the Playing Field

Writing in *Campaign Magazine,* media trainer Karen Kalish (1996) called every media interview "a glorious opportunity to get your point across. It's a chance for exposure and free advertising, to inform the public, to clear up misconceptions, and to put your work in the public's mind" (p. 44).

Working with the news media should be on the agenda of every psychologist as psychology and behavioral science fight for appropriate consumer recognition and their fair share of the research pie. But also compulsory when doing news media interviews is preparation.

The Preinterview Phase

From the interviewee's perspective, one of the most important pieces of the interview process is the "interview before the interview." This preinterview process is when the news source gets to ask the questions. Here's what you will want to know:

1. What news outlet is the reporter calling from? If you're unfamiliar with it, ask more questions. What is its format (e.g., newspaper, magazine, radio, TV spot news, TV magazine news)? Is the show live or taped? If live, is there an audience? Does the show take telephone call-ins from listeners? What is its length? Its frequency? Who are the other guests?

2. What's the theme of the story, or in what direction does the reporter think the story is moving? What information is the reporter looking to you to provide? If the reporter says "I am really just beginning to talk to some people about this," it is a golden opportunity for you. It may require a bit more time on your part, but it's an opportunity to really educate the reporter and therefore have more influence on the story than any other news source.

3. Who else has the reporter spoken to or has plans to speak to? (This information can often give you a clue as to the direction or bias of the story.)

4. If you're being asked to appear on a broadcast show, pay extra attention to the show's format. What you want to avoid is being asked to participate in what is being set up to be a heated debate or being asked to solve the complex problems of another guest in the last 30 seconds of the show.

Once you have asked these questions and gotten answers, it is time to decide whether you feel you are the right person to do the interview. If the answer is yes, agree on a time that the reporter can call you back or come to your office to do the interview. Keep in mind the reporter's time pressures. The earlier in the process the reporter gets your information and point of view, the better he or she can synthesize the information into the story in its appropriate context. Remember, at this point in the process you also have the right to set some ground rules as to where the interview will take place and how long the interview will last. Being generous with your time in helping a reporter learn about and understand the subject area makes sense, but spending hours with him or her does not. A good length of time for a typical phone interview is 15–20 minutes; for an in-person interview, 45 minutes to 1 hour.

Preparing for the Interview

Having a goal for the interview and knowing the words and phrases you will use to express your knowledge and point of view are critical to its success. Preparing brief summaries of your research or clinical work is a good way to help you frame your message, but also gives you a valuable overview you can share with reporters to help them prepare as well.

Before the interview begins, create the three most important message points you want to communicate. Write them out. Practice them. Are they credible, simple without being simplistic, brief and true to your expertise and the psychological literature? It is also important to give some thought to the questions you are likely to be asked and, of course, what your answers will be. But don't assume that every question the reporter asks is the right question. Some will be the wrong question based on the reporter's lack of understanding of the subject area or a reporter who is fishing for controversy. It is important to acknowledge a reporter's question but also to correct it if it is based on a false premise. Then bridge away from it if it leads you away from the messages that you want to deliver.

The following are examples of bridge phases:

- □ "The real issue is . . . "
- □ "What's important to remember is . . . "
- □ "I don't know the answer to that question, but what I do know is . . . "
- □ "The main point here is . . . "
- □ "The bottom line here is . . . "

During the Interview

At best, you can control the tempo and pace of the interview by keeping your answers brief and avoiding the temptation to fill all the time with your voice. Silence between questions should not make you nervous; it gives both you and the reporter time to think.

Reporters are fond of asking a few questions at one time and are known to interrupt frequently. When faced with multiple questions and an aggressive reporter, it is important to keep your cool. Break down multipronged questions and deal with one issue at a time. When stuck about how to respond or where to go next, remember the message points that you crafted and want to deliver. Returning to your message points will help you get back on track if you feel an interview is going awry (see exhibit 1).

After the Interview

Evaluating Your Performance. We are often our own worst critics, especially when it comes to seeing our image on television or hearing our voice on the radio. However, the best way to evaluate your performance is to ask yourself the question, Did I deliver my three message points, and did they get into the story in an appropriate context? The only issues you should concern yourself with in terms of how you look or sound is if your appearance, body language, or voice got in the way of the audience hearing your message. Such questions as, Did I mumble or speak too rapidly? Did I look disinterested or nervous? and Was my loud tie a distraction? are all appropriate.

What to Do When You Are Unhappy With a Story. Very rarely is a news report everything you would have wanted it to be if you had written it yourself. What is important to focus on is the big picture. What broad theme or message is received by the reader or viewer? Remember that it takes many, many impressions over time to influence public opinion. Consider your interview one small piece of that larger effort.

Occasionally news sources feel that they were misquoted by a reporter and want to demand a correction. There are times when it is appropriate to ask for such a correction, but there are also times when making such a request can backfire. When a factual error appears in a news story, it is fair and appropriate to ask for a correction. Do so firmly but nicely. Remember that journalists are people, too, and therefore subject to the same issues of ego and anger as everyone else. (What's different, however, is that news people control what will be reported on tomorrow. You do not.) It also will be important to make the correction in future interviews on the subject. Reporters often use old news clips as a way to brief themselves on a topic. If a reporter's question is based on a false premise, tell them so and explain why.

When you feel that the story for which you were a news source has missed a particular context or nuance, this is not necessarily the time to demand a correction. One risk of doing so is that you put yourself and your organization at risk of being perceived by the editor or reporter as protesting too much, and that can beget an embarrassing second-day news story, or a less than friendly reporter the next time you are involved in a news event. The preceding discussion is summarized in Exhibit 1.

Closing Thoughts

Working with the news media is an important means by which psychologists and behavioral scientists educate the public about the value of their work. Interviews are the primary means by which news is gathered. The news media and psychologists have important things to offer each other. News media relations, however, should be approached with a degree of caution and lots of preparation. Psychologists who are interested in working with the news media should avail themselves of media-training workshops and seminars offered by APA and other entities. As long as marketplace issues have the potential to impact the study and application

Exhibit 1

Preinterview strategies:

☐ Do your homework.
☐ Anticipate key questions.
☐ Prepare key answers, including quotable phrases.
☐ Prepare and fine-tune your three message points.

Your rights during the interview:

☐ To determine the approximate length of the interview.
☐ To select where you want to be interviewed.
☐ To ask in advance for the topics to be covered during the interview. (Occasionally reporters will give you a copy of the questions they would like to ask. But this doesn't happen often, and if you do get such a list, don't assume that the interview will not stray from that list.)
☐ To set your own pace in answering questions. Don't let the reporter rush you. Taking time to think before responding to a question is a good idea.
☐ To correct false premises and challenge questionable assertions or assumptions.

Your job during the interview:

☐ To deliver your message points in brief, understandable, quotable language.
☐ To speak in plain English and avoid jargon.
☐ To speak within the range of your knowledge, and to not be afraid to say, "I don't know."
☐ To be positive, not defensive. To use bridges to move away from topics you do not want to talk about and to your message points.
☐ To keep the reporter from putting words in your mouth or creating controversy when none exists.

of psychology and human behavior, educating the public through the news media about the value of psychology will continue to be an important public relations tool for the discipline. For more information about APA's referral service or to request a membership application, contact the APA Public Affairs Office at (202) 336-5700 or by electronic mail to publiccom@apa.org.

References

American Psychological Association, Public Information Committee. (1996). *Draft guidelines for psychologists working with the news media* (8th ed.). Washington, DC: Author.

Foundation for American Communications. (1990). *Media resource guide: How to tell your story* (5th ed.). Alexandria, VA: Foundation for American Communications.

Kalish, K. (1996, June). Meeting the press on your terms. *Campaign Magazine,* 44–46.

Public Relations Society of America. (1996, April). Stories editors are looking for. *Public Relations Tactics,* 9.

Rafe, S. C., & Pfister, W. J. (1983, August). The art of the interview. *VideoPro,* 54–58.

Sherman, S. P. (1989, June 19). Smart ways to handle the press. *Fortune,* 69–75.

2

So You Want to Work in the Media? 21 Things I Wish I Had Known When I First Asked Myself That Question

Michael S. Broder

My rather intense involvement with the media came about quite by accident. Over 20 years ago, I was trying to figure out ways to get participants for my dissertation study, which was on divorce adjustment. Unlike many research projects where subjects can be obtained from intact groups (e.g., the good old Intro Psych class), getting people to enter a program designed to help them overcome the pain of ending a love relationship wasn't so easy. A friend suggested that I send public service announcements to all of the Philadelphia-area radio stations in the hope they would announce that an experimental, free program was available to those who met the criteria and agreed to fully participate. I needed 50 qualified participants and was running out of ideas. So practically as a last effort before switching topics, I gave it a try.

The only responses I got were from the two Philadelphia talk radio stations, asking me if I wanted to be a guest on one of their shows discussing the topic of divorce, in general, and my program, in specific. In the late 1970s, they actually thought this was a unique and provocative topic. How quaint were those presensationalism days of the media!

At first, I had serious reservations. Rarely, if ever, had I even listened to talk radio. Moreover, I knew of no one at the time who had ever exposed himself or herself to this ordeal. But, hell, I was desperate for participants. So I accepted both invitations—a decision that was to radically change my life, not to mention my career direction, forever.

To make a very long story as short as possible, I got my subjects, managed to get both of the stations that invited me upset (for appearing on these rival talk stations on the same day with virtually the same pitch), and—still unwittingly—began what was to become perhaps the most unique and intense part of my career. In the years since, I've had my own programs on both of those local Philadelphia stations, hosted talk shows for all three major networks (CBS Radio, ABC Talkradio, and NBC Talknet), in addition to New York City's two major local talk stations, and made numerous guest appearances on such programs as the *Today Show*, *Oprah Winfrey*, *Donahue*, *Sally Jessy Raphael* and (even) *Geraldo*, as well as on hundreds of other shows. I have written popular articles or have been featured in numerous national, regional, and local publications, including *Newsweek*, *USA Today*, *New York Times*, and *Cosmopolitan* (and scores of others); have written two popular self-help books, *The Art of Living Single* (Broder & Claflin, 1990) and *The Art of Staying Together* (Broder, 1994), 14 popular audio self-help programs, and *The Therapist's Assistant™*, the only audiotherapy series designed to be used by psychotherapists with clients as an adjunct to treatment; and have completed five multicity media–book tours in the United States and Australia.

Radio psychologists were being villified by our colleagues in the early 1980s for daring to give advice over the airwaves. In 1982, a group of us radio psychologists, along with other psychologists who worked in or were interested in media issues, met in San Diego, CA. It was at that meeting that we actually coined the term *media psychology* and formed the Association for Media Psychology (AMP), which was to become the precursor to the American Psychological Association's (APA's) Division of Media Psychology (Division 46), of which I became the first president. The story of AMP and Division 46 has been told many times. Our mission was to pool our resources and work together with several purposes in mind: to educate the public about the profession of psychology and how it can serve them; to refine our media skills and teach these skills to our colleagues wanting to utilize this new specialty as part of their work; to be both a consumer and a source of media-related research; to develop *Guidelines for Media Mental Health Professionals* (Broder, 1983); to be a sort of a guild and source of ongoing support for those of us who worked in the media; and to be a clearinghouse for media opportunities, as well as a resource for the media when they were looking for psychologists to fulfill various media roles. Interestingly, media lawyers are now going through similar struggles—which started with the O.J. Simpson trial, continued with the Clinton scandals, and seem to be here to stay. They are now very much where we were in the 1980s. (And wasn't Monica Lewinsky's early lawyer, William Ginsburg, the very caricature of the worst and most outrageous media behavior we shuddered about back then?)

The degree to which these goals were met is very much a matter of opinion and beyond the scope of this chapter. But I can best describe it as a mission in progress. I think of those early (AMP/Division 46) days with a great deal of pride and nostalgia. And as lowbrow as the media gets, you'll never hear me suggest that we censor anything! The initial controversy of it all is what got me hooked. Once media psychology gained the acceptance and professional respect it deserved, I found myself becoming less and less engaged on an organizational level. I choose to no longer do radio on a regular basis, although I will occasionally guest host. I still do a great deal of writing—books, articles, and tape programs (my most passionate professional activity)—and make guest appearances on radio and television as it pertains to that work.

Along the way, there were many lessons about working in the media to be learned. Some were formulated naturally, whereas others needed to be learned the hard way. So let me share some of the ones that I and other media psychologists who have consulted with me over the years have considered most important. In doing that, let me emphasize that this is strictly my own perspective. I claim no absolute truth here, only opinion and learning-based experiences that would have been quite helpful to know at the beginning. In other words, what follows is the article I wish had been available for me to read 20 years ago:

1. *The debate of whether advice given over the airwaves is therapy or infotainment was always a ridiculous argument.* Therapy is not done over the airwaves simply because it *cannot be done* over the airwaves. Never be defensive about the fact that when you are working in radio or TV (which in this country is pretty much commercially funded) that you are working for an entertainment medium. Sure, media psychologists (both print and radio/TV) have educated the public on how to normalize such things as relationship, career, and child rearing issues. Media psychologists have taught those who have needed to handle contemporary issues such as agoraphobia, bulimia, addiction, and even sexual harassment (pre-Anita Hill and Clarence Thomas) that they are not alone. Those of us who have succeeded in the media have done so mainly because we have been able to entertain and thus keep what is perhaps the most uncaptive audience you can have watching, listening, or reading. Many of the points to come will crystallize various aspects of this theme.

2. *A career in the media can be akin to professional cyclothymia.* Working on the air is often both an incredibly exhilarating and profoundly addictive experience. At its best, the pay is inordinately high; speaking engagements can be quite plentiful; the recognition, both professional and otherwise, is intense; and the pressure that often manifests itself as glorious excitement can bring one's creative juices to levels never before imagined! At worst, I have often compared it to the phenomenon of being in love with someone whom you don't particularly like. As trends change, more sensationalism is first suggested, then requested, then demanded. All of the clichés you saw in the movies (e.g., *Network* and *Broadcast News*, which some would say actually sweeten the characters greatly) are accurate. Media psychologists have been endlessly (and often rightfully) parodied, both consciously and unconsciously. Since the invention of the TelePrompTer, TV hosts and newspeople with few exceptions have needed less

and less substance (other than that ability to read their Tele-PrompTer) but more and more appeal to survive. Television talk shows (and radio is not far behind), once a glorious showcase for what we do, have grown sleazier and sleazier, and survival means constantly redefining yourself and your "act." (As Charles Manson once said, "There was a time when being crazy meant something; now everyone's crazy!") Remember, the same demographics that made Arthur Godfrey the nation's leading morning man in the 1940s and 1950s (who today would be lucky to be working steadily in Toledo, Ohio) now overwhelmingly listen to Howard Stern!

3. *It's the ratings, stupid.* Or to parody a real estate cliché, there are only three things that the media consider important: ratings, ratings, and ratings! Remember Phil Donahue? He's a great guy and did a great show. But when his ratings dropped, he was unceremoniously dumped after $29^1/_2$ years of carrying the daytime bottom line of many of his affiliate stations on his shoulders (they wouldn't even let him stay around for his 30th). By contrast, the Jerry Seinfelds and the Ellen DeGenereses could publicly make outrageous demands to their employers and still keep their time slots—but only until they wanted out or their ratings dropped! If you wonder why this has become the age of the telegenic sociopath (e.g., O. J. Simpson, Donald Trump, Tonya Harding, and Bill Clinton), you need look no further than the rating books. So it's not how nice, professional, smart, loyal, helpful, or thorough you are, but how well you attract numbers of people. Size—and ultimately little else—matters! By thinking of the media establishments for whom we work as businesses and not institutions of higher learning (a common tactical error many psychologists still make), we will practically always have our eye on the ball.

4. *This journey is peppered with some of the most fascinating characters you'll ever meet.* In my media career, I have run into some of the most interesting, accomplished, evolved, and humble, as well as some of the most boring, pathetic, shoddy, and ego-driven, Axis II types I've ever met anywhere! Few novelists could create some of the actual characters that await you. By observing it and constantly fine-tuning my level of

involvement, this phenomenon has greatly broadened my overall perspective as a psychologist. I consider this a huge and unexpected bonus of my media career.

5. *Understand the nature of a media relationship.* There is an unwritten contract that says they use you for your expertise or to lend your credentials to a point of view they want to express. In turn, you use them for your purposes. When guesting, they will invariably look at you as a one-shot deal. The mistake that many psychologists make is to consider a guest appearance as an audition for something greater. Instead, if *you* treat everything like a one-shot deal and then give it your best shot, you will probably convey a much greater sense of confidence. Chances are you don't know their full agenda in having you as a guest. For example, the producer of one program called me recently to ask if I knew of a female psychologist, preferably with a "non-Catholic" (read: not Irish or Italian) name who was pro-life! I don't know if the show ever found one. But if they did, I can guarantee you that this psychologist did not realize that their agenda was probably to set her up for some kind of attack. As individuals, psychologists (with rare exceptions) are not important to those in the media who pursue them. That is not necessarily a bad thing, as long as we stay aware of it.

6. *A great guest has five characteristics.* Great guests have passion for and about whatever he or she is addressing; a sense of humor; clarity (the ability to explain a complicated issue, such as Maslow's needs hierarchy, to an 11th grader with a short attention span); a definite opinion or point of view about the topic; and a chip on the shoulder. Many psychologists have the hardest time with that chip-on-shoulder characteristic. But watch the professional guests, such as when Larry King is interviewed by David Letterman (or vice versa), or whenever you see Ruth Westheimer on a talk show. She is extremely pleasant, but never, ever wishy-washy. In other words, regardless of your unique style, always come out with your dukes up!

7. *Learn to make it look easy.* But don't expect it to be easy. The appearance of ease while operating at peak performance is not a simple skill to develop. But with thorough prepara-

tion and a great deal of practice, it will eventually become second nature. The opposite, of course, is to look like you're trying to audition. The camera and the microphone are very sensitive instruments. So expect that whatever anxiety you project will become greatly magnified. Granted, some anxiety is actually good for peak performance, as long as it doesn't show and you can reframe it to come across as excitement (read: passion).

8. *Think of your media appearance as the exact opposite of your dissertation.* A dissertation can take as few as one or two very simple points and expand them into a study that can be many hundreds of pages long. In working with the media, your task is the exact opposite. You must take very complex subjects, such as marital communication, stepparenting, or eating disorders, and then reduce them to sound bites or vignettes that can be readily understood by your composite audience (that individual with an 11th grade education and the short attention span). You can try this simple exercise at home: Take your dissertation topic and explain it in 30 seconds or less to someone who has virtually no interest either in you, your topic, or psychology. Then once you've mastered that 30-second task, realize that the average sound bite on news or magazine shows today is about 7 seconds. And remember, the easier it is to change stations (and the more stations there are to change to), the less captive is your audience.

9. *Know as much as you can about what you're getting yourself into.* Before making an appearance, get as much information about the show, the host, the format, other guests with whom you may be expected to interact, and the worst possible situation you can be exposed to during your appearance. Is the show controversial? Is it informational? Is it a forum for puffery? Are the producers after sensationalism? Is the host respectful of professionals, or are you merely there to be a foil or even a stooge? All of these scenarios can be worked to your advantage as long as you understand within reason what to expect. Shortly after I completed my U.S. paperback tour for *The Art of Staying Together* (Broder, 1994), in which most of the shows were interested in discussing things such as sex, affairs, abusive relationships, and the other more pro-

vocative topics in the book, I toured in Australia. Their talk shows were quite reminiscent of ours in the 1960s and 1970s. Hosts asked questions such as, "How does a marriage stay together?" without the now-routine American embellishments such as "if one partner is 50 years older than the other?" This was culture shock! By the second day, I caught on, but I must admit I was quite unprepared at first!

10. *These three skills will help you greatly*: Improvisational acting (where you will learn to fine-tune your persona for practically any given situation), voice (where you will learn how to make the best possible vocal presentation by changing certain quirks that might get in your way—and we all have them), and bringing yourself to a peak-performance state of mind at will. The latter will ensure that you're at optimal energy level before you go on the air. This is especially important when you're on a media tour that requires you to make numerous appearances on a given day. Media tours can be quite grueling, because the days are usually long and appearances can be both numerous and spaced out unevenly. Improvisational acting and voice training are best obtained by professional coaches and classes that are generally available locally.

11. *Breaking into the media can be difficult, but it is not impossible.* This subject is a book in and of itself. Quite obviously, the better the opportunity, the more competition there is. Master guesting before attempting to host. With very few exceptions, well paying positions are now almost impossible to get without a solid talent agent. In selecting an agent, make sure he or she has a track record in placing people similar to you in the medium you are looking for. Rarely does someone break in without a great deal of conscious effort, which includes sending out numerous tapes and bios, taking auditions, handling rejections, and once again never allowing it to become too important. Some of the best media gigs are actually created by those who seek them. In other words, if you can develop a win–win airtight proposal with sources for funding, you're in the best possible position to have it looked at by the right people and then to eventually succeed. A station or network that has already created a position simply awaiting talent is more or less an exception to the rule.

And when such a situation does occur, the talent they select will practically always be someone who has a solid track record of delivering ratings.

12. *Remember the audience.* No matter what medium you are working in—and I'll have a few words about the three most specific ones: radio, television, and print—remember that the most important element is your audience. It is the audience who decides whether you stay or go; it is your audience who pays your salary. When appearing on a show, it is not the host that you're interacting with. The host is merely a catalyst to bring you to the audience. Likewise, when doing radio call-in programs, it is not the caller that the program exists for, but the audience. Your caller is merely the instrument to bring your message to the listeners. (You're not running a crisis hotline!) So constantly ask yourself, "How does what I say or do benefit or impact the audience?" and you'll just about always be on the right track.

13. *In radio what you say is all you have—that's good news and bad news.* We still hear over and over again about the Kennedy–Nixon television debates in 1960, where Kennedy clearly won on TV. But what we hear less about is that those who listened to the debates on the radio overwhelmingly thought Nixon won. In radio, although you don't have to worry about what your audience sees, what your audience sees won't get you out of trouble either. Pauses are called "dead air." A big advantage of radio is that there is usally much more time. Thus, you can generally get into a lot more depth and use your notes as much as you need or want to. Another aspect of radio is that your show must be structured so that someone can tune in at any time and feel as though they're on board—unlike television.

14. *In television, the "eyes" have it.* Unlike radio, unless you're using a TelePrompTer, your main points must be memorized. You generally have much less time but are expected to at least appear to convey the same level of depth you would anywhere else. This is quite a challenge. In addition, about 80% of the "grade" for your presentation is visual. This means that you can make a brilliant point, but if the camera is focusing on someone else's facial reaction to what you're saying, chances are your point will be lost and

that facial reaction—if anything—will be remembered. Make sure that how you dress as well as other aspects of your appearance reinforce your message. At the very least, your appearance should not detract from or be inconsistent with your message.

15. *Just one short word about print media.* Writers' Market (Holm & Prues, 1997) is a book that comes out every year and details virtually every publishing (book and magazine) resource that might be appropriate for your work. This fine publication will give you information about how to write query letters (for articles and books) and find book agents and how virtually anyone with both a good product and perseverance can get published. If you truly have something to say, this is by far the easiest medium to break into and the one that is most likely to propel you into the media in this day and age (by virtue of appearances for your books and articles and the prominence in your area of expertise your writings will establish for you).

16. *Print interviews, such as for newspapers and magazines, are also good ways to gain recognition by other media sources.* Unlike the radio and TV (when you just about always know when you're on the air), be conscious of never speaking "off the record." Watch for the old "Columbo" technique where the reporter says to you after you think the interview is completed, "Oh, just one more thing . . ." and you begin to answer as though you are off the record, only to find that whatever you said at that moment is the only thing that appears in print. A very small minority of extraordinarily gracious reporters and publications (as well as a few who are reeling from lawsuits) will clear your quote with you before publication. This is the exception, not the rule, so don't expect this courtesy. Just be careful that your words are appropriately measured.

17. *Consciously develop your media persona.* In therapy, we use protocols. Theoretically we could say the same thing over and over again many times during the course of a day without sounding (to anyone else) repetitious. And theoretically, one could do great therapy without ever using any type of original approach. But in the media it is uniqueness that counts. Uniqueness not so much about what you say, but

about how you come across. So remember to be not only an authority but also a character or personality. Virtually any media person you can think of has some distinct physical or personality characteristic that is a trademark—even if it is something really subtle like "dryness." Chances are this was developed after a great deal of thought and practice—even though it may still be a staple of his or her personality. Think about what persona you can convey comfortably and naturally that can be chosen to enhance your message. Then do what it takes to incorporate that persona into whatever you do with consistency.

18. *Know your goals.* What is driving your media work? If it is to convey your message, you can always find a forum, a classroom, an article, a small radio station, or another outlet to use as a launching point. On the other hand, if your goal is to *be* something, such as a celebrity (versus to say or accomplish something), the media can be a very frustrating experience. Amid the snickering heard at a recent APA convention about a colleague who believed that one more face-lift would get her that "TV job" and some much needed self-esteem, there is a very sad dynamic that characterizes those who hunger for stardom. Although there are an infinite number of electronic and print opportunities, there are very few star slots. Furthermore, the star slots that do exist are invariably occupied by those who have painstakingly paid their dues and developed substance along with their act. Narcissism or arrogance without talent will get you only as far as the first exit door. Thus, the best chance you have of assuring yourself of a positive experience is to concentrate on your message (the means) and not the size of your audience (which is the result of good work, not the means). If your message and delivery works, your audience will invariably increase. I've observed that those who have the most difficulty really have not adequately concentrated on and fine-tuned their message (i.e., made it valuable) and then expect a lot of recognition for having little new to say. But when you truly have something fresh, important, and helpful to say, there will be plenty of people to listen.

19. *What we do in our offices is far more consequential.* There used to be a debate about whether we who did radio call-in

programs actually helped callers. After 17 years of doing radio, I believe that we probably are helpful, but not nearly as much as we thought we were. Do we hurt them? No. I've never seen or heard of a true victim. But I have seen many colleagues make a lot more of what they considered their effect and the effect of media psychology than I did. I believe I make a much deeper and far-reaching contribution, albeit to fewer numbers of people per minute, when I conduct continuing education seminars, teach clinical courses, and see clients in my office.

20. *Only do what is fun.* And when it stops being fun, stop doing it! That's when both Jack Paar and Johnny Carson left the "Tonight Show," and practically every one I have met who has had an overall positive experience with the media has adopted that attitude. It is the only truism I can think of which guarantees that you become a winner in this game, no matter what.

21. *Finally, don't take yourself too seriously!* For 17 years, I have ended every radio show with that message! And believe it or not, that mantra was never more applicable than when I was president of Division 46 and also acted as the "unofficial chief bereavement counselor" for those who lost their shows. At that time, I got a lot of experience administering the "Rambo" technique of coping: Ignore the pain, and you will survive it. Then what is left is that great feeling of having reached many people for a moment in time.

References

Broder, M. S. (1983). *Guidelines for media mental health professionals*, with Guidelines Committee of the Association for Media Psychology.

Broder, M. S. (1994). *The art of staying together.* New York: Avon Books.

Broder, M. S., & Claflin, E. B. (1990). *The art of living single: A complete guide to enjoying life on your own.* New York: Avon Books.

Holm, K. C., & Prues, D. (1997). *Writers market.* Cincinnati, OH: Writers Digest Books.

3

Working With the Media:
The Person and the Persona

Dan Gottlieb With Lita Linzer Schwartz

Dan Gottlieb works primarily in radio and print in addition to having a private practice. He presents a weekly broadcast (*Voices in the Family*) on the public broadcasting station (WHYY—91FM) in Philadelphia and writes a semi-monthly newspaper column ("On Healing") in the *Philadelphia Inquirer*. His comments here are focused, in part, on the differences in working with these two media and, in part, on how psychologists can use the media more effectively. After the interview, a brief reference list is provided of articles that focus on Gottlieb, or on other psychologists in the news as media persons. The Appendix lists several of Gottlieb's articles, so that the reader can appreciate the range of topics he has covered. His contribution is in interview format not because interviews are an integral part of the media, but for reasons related to Dan's health, which will become apparent shortly.

> **Lita:** Dan, how long have you been doing your column and your broadcasts?
>
> **Dan:** I've been doing broadcasts since 1985 and the column in the *Philadelphia Inquirer* since 1993, so, as we speak, it's been 13 years on the radio and 5 for the column.

Lita: What pushed you in the direction of the media?

Dan: It was clearly my accident. On December 20, 1979, when I was a 33-year-old psychologist, I was in an automobile accident that severed my cervical spine. At that instant, I became a quadriplegic. The most devastating effect of my accident was my alienation; I felt disconnected from friends and even family. They looked at me differently. To bridge the gap between me and the rest of the world, I needed to explain what I felt like inside; it was the only way to combat my sense of alienation. Now at the time, nobody had ever done that. Most quadriplegics were kids who had broken their necks in auto accidents or gang wars and were not verbal. Not only was I older and verbal, but I was a psychologist, so that I could describe my feelings in fairly accurate and comprehensive detail. So I began, right from the beginning, telling my story, and the doctors were really taken aback.

Some of my colleagues wanted me to dictate my experience, and they called Darrell Sifford [then a columnist for the *Philadelphia Inquirer*]. He wrote a column about it. He was quite moved by my story, as I was by him. It was a story essentially of pain, of alienation, of depression, and of grief. But, it was also a story of tenacity and perseverance in the face of fear. When he published it in March of 1980, for the first time, I felt I had reclaimed the voice I never had. The article was extremely well received, and he published several more thereafter [Sifford, 1982].

In 1984, my depression was at its worst. With most traumas like mine, the first several years are spent learning a new identity and lifestyle. It is only then that the sense of loss and depression sets in. For the first time in my life, I experienced a major depression and was barely functional. Compounding the problem, I was facing my 40th birthday with what felt like a bleak future, and my marriage was rapidly deteriorating.

In February of that year, I was invited by Marty Moss-Coane, then the producer of *Family Matters* on the local PBS station, to be a guest on her show. There was something about that show, a show on marriage and intimacy ... that evening was magical.

Lita: I can imagine. It gave you a whole new perspective, perhaps? Or another outlet?

Dan: I think one of the things that made it magical was my relationship with the callers. Up until then, the show had been a question and answer format. When I was the guest, I treated the callers with more respect and emotional contact. I asked them questions about their lives rather than simply giving them answers. This type of approach was unprecedented at the time.

Three months later, Marty called and said she wanted to talk with me, and I had some idea what it was about. Now every psychologist in the country will probably say that with everything going on in my life that would have been the worst time to make a serious career-changing decision. But when she offered me the show, I instantly said yes. Never, ever, was I so terrified! For 2 weeks, I couldn't take a deep breath. To finally answer your question, it was not a conscious choice to get into the media; it was a conspiracy of events that got me there.

I even feel that some of the events were spiritual in nature. After all, I needed to find my voice in my pursuit of wholeness. And here I was, being handed a microphone! Perhaps coincidence and perhaps not.

Lita: When I've been on your show, I've noticed a real feeling of intimacy from our callers. How do you do this?

Dan: My vision, when I'm on the air, is that there are about 8 to 10 people listening, which gives me a real feeling of intimacy.

Lita: I know that you have *many* listeners to your broadcasts. This must be a source of great satisfaction to you. But have you had any significantly strong responses to specific programs over the years, either positive or negative?

Dan: One of the most powerful shows I ever did was after I was on the air about 6 months. My vision in my terror was that all my listeners had PhDs in psychology from Ivy League schools. Remember that what I carried in was a tremendous depression and insecurity about my disability. In my own prejudiced mind, I thought that if they knew I was a quadriplegic, I would lose credibility and therefore be seen as incompetent. Part of that was projection, and part of it was that that was 13 years ago, and there was a different vision of the disabled then. So I did the first shows in fear of being discovered.

Then we did a show on disabilities. Teddy Pendergass was my guest, and that was the first show where I opened up about being a quadriplegic. I talked about my fears, wishes, and feelings of alienation. The response was incredible. Not only were the calls from the outside supportive and grateful, but the callers were open, vulnerable, and intimate. It was as though my vulnerability finally gave them permission to speak out.

Shortly thereafter we did an open show in which I had no guests. That was the single most emotionally powerful show that I've ever done. The callers were as open about their feelings as a patient who had been in therapy for 6 months. From there on, I opened up about my feelings, my fears, and my visions, so my audience did, too. My projection since then has shifted 180 degrees, so that now my vision of my role is that people come to me with enough trust and respect to ask me to listen. Everyone that dials that phone on the air . . . every light blinking— I feel honored. They trust me and have contributed significantly to the quality and meaning of my life. I attempt to communicate this gratitude to them. That's not technique. Those are feelings. And I feel a sense of responsibility to them, too. It's important that these are feelings and not techniques.

Lita: I've noticed this trust on the part of your callers and their willingness to express their deepest feelings. Your revelation of yourself comes through in your columns as well as on the air, and that's difficult to do in print. When it is oral, that's easier, as you can get the intonation in the voice. Print is . . . just black on white.

Dan: I feel the same way that you do. I think others find it easier in print. To me, the word—the spoken word— is so much easier. I feel so much more accountable.

Lita: Well, you can't take words back, and you can't erase them, which is something that I try to teach people for other reasons. What about responses to your *Inquirer* columns, because there is no "call-in" possibility with those? I have noted that you sometimes mention that a specific column is in response to a reader's question or comment.

Dan: Some weeks I'll get close to 20 letters. That's the most that I'll get. Some weeks, I'll get none. And I'm told that it's widely read. If I write a column about somebody, or some program, they will always say they got 30 or 50 calls. I do get feedback, but it's less predictable than from the radio show.

Lita: It appears that some of your columns are in response to letters. Some are clearly with reference to things important to you, like death and illness. Do you have special reasons for some of your columns? In October of 1997, for example, you wrote one on the rising tide of juvenile violence. Was that in response to the murder of the boy collecting for the PTA (a local case) or because of juvenile violence itself?

Dan: Let me check. That was in response to a report from the Centers for Disease Control.

Lita: In some of these other articles, you really talk to your audience. It's not preaching; it's having a conversation.

Dan: I worry about it if it sounds preachy. What I do is share what I've learned. We don't turn our backs on hatred; but we do turn our backs on the suffering that gives birth to hatred. Some columns are written in response to letters; some in response to new information. I try to share my knowledge and thoughts with the readers.

Lita: To what extent do you think media psychologists should reveal themselves as people? You have certainly referred to your own life from time to time in columns and on the air, for example, when your mother died or when you realized how some of your perceptions affected your reaction to certain other people. How far do you go with this? Certainly there are questions about the practice of some psychologists revealing too much of themselves, that that's not good. They feel that you should keep your distance from your patients.

Dan: Hiding oneself from patients is what used to be

done. Nothing could be more disrespectful to a patient. Now I'm going to take a step aside from media for a minute and talk about psychotherapeutic relationships. Many of my patients come with their psychopathologies, but they also come in with diminished self-esteem, with a life that has lost meaning. They come into my office, and as a result of their presence, they contribute to the meaning of my life. But my presence does not contribute to the meaning of theirs. Now what I try to communicate to them is my gratitude for what they have done for me.

I want to add to that thought about self-disclosure. Years ago, what self-disclosure meant was that I would say to a patient, "This is the way I did it," and "This is the way I mastered it." That's not self-disclosure; that's self-serving. It's also a lie. To me, self-disclosure is talking about your vulnerability and your confusion. I've learned this lesson from two places.

One of my first experiences in the media goes back many years ago. I was invited to be a guest on a Saturday afternoon kids' show. Someone was invited as an "expert" every Saturday. I forget what I was an expert on that day; it might have been drugs. My wife was watching, and I was only 28, 29 years old myself. One of the kids asked me a question about drug abuse, and I said, "I don't know. I really don't know. I'll tell you what. I'll give you my phone number and you give me yours. I'll look it up and we'll talk Monday."

Now when I said this on the air, I didn't think anything of it, but the engineer sitting in the booth next to my wife was shocked. He said, "What a wonderful moment! I've never before heard an expert say that. We've never heard an expert say those three words: 'I don't know.'" It was wonderful permission for me that I could do that, but I never knew it was okay to do that.

Lita: I think we were all sort of brainwashed. Freud would never have said "I don't know," and many of his followers would not have.

Dan: No, he wouldn't have. To me, self-disclosure allows us to say "I don't know" or "That's an issue I struggle with" and "I've wrestled with that." It's not the details that are important, because they're not interested in that, just like they don't want to hear about "When I was a boy, I walked 20 miles to school . . ."

Lita: What impact do you think psychologists' broadcasts and columns have in general, Dan? . . . I guess I'm kind of concerned about impact because not all of them are as straight as you're being. Can you give an example or two?

Dan: I think too many mental health professionals sell out when it comes to the media. The media says to one of us, "I need a quick simple answer in a 60-second sound bite," and we do it. We can always find that answer. And we can always find a theory that will justify any answer on any side of any issue.

Lita: Now, how about some of the others? The one I hear about is Dr. Laura. What about those who misuse the microphone? For example, I've seen two recent articles about Dr. Laura. [Note: For those who are unfamiliar with Dr. Laura, she is not a psychologist but has a PhD in physiology and is a licensed marriage, family, and child counselor in California (Wylie, 1997). She is described as "the acerbic call-in 'shrink' who urges callers to take responsibility for their personal problems" (DeAngelis, 1997, p. 10).]

Dan: As to Dr. Laura, she is extremely judgmental. It's interesting. She's on target clinically, usually. I often agree with her answers, but she lacks empathy, she doesn't care about the feelings of the people who call. Even though the content of what she advises is not necessarily wrong, she'll say something like "Don't be a wimp! Cut this guy off." I, on the other hand, will encourage somebody to look inside and understand what their tolerance is, what they need to be a better person in and out of this relationship. But she doesn't care about that apparently. She's got a vision of a way of handling life. Granted there are certain truths in life, but when we force patients into our value system, it's unethical.

Lita: Maybe some of the callers get some kind of psychic reward from the attention, even though it's abuse of a kind.

Dan: True. The same question comes up with the *Jerry Springer* show.

Lita: If we turn away from your own show for a moment, what do you think is the impact of some of the high-profile TV shows where people's allegedly innermost secrets are revealed or they are confronted with someone they haven't seen in years (or possibly ever)? For example, a woman gave up a son for adoption, never told her husband, and is suddenly confronted on screen with a 32-year-old son. Is this or some of the other shows that are even more confrontational doing harm? What about the audience's reaction?

Dan: I have very strong feelings about this. I would hope that any psychologist in the media would be careful about the talk and tabloid shows. Let me explain. It's this "we/they" mentality, where the talk shows say, "Let's look at those freaks. Let *us* sit back and look at *those* freaks." We're looking at women who sell their children for prostitution or have silicone breast implants. . . . "Let's look at those freaks." That mentality encourages the audience in its denial and dissociation. It helps the audience to say, "I am not you. That is, the farther I can get away from you, the more I can humiliate you or laugh at you, the better I am, the more self-esteem I have."

It's almost a kind of entertainment to laugh at other people. I have always tried to do the opposite. We will do a diagnostic show, and my goal is always to leave the audience with something that shows what we have in common.

We did a show on obesity where my guest was a woman who weighed 400 lbs. The audience understood the suffering this woman had, walking into a restaurant, eating a meal in public, of being hated just for being the woman she is. That's just the opposite of what would happen if she went on one of the tabloid shows. I try to find commonalities between us rather than play the aggressor.

Lita: That must have been difficult, because they weren't *seeing* the woman over the radio.

Dan: It's interesting, Lita. I talk about making eye contact. I try to make eye contact even on the radio, but I don't do it as real radio professionals would. They would describe the woman. I try using a more conversational approach, a more one-on-one approach. That allows me to make the eye contact, which is my goal. That's what I do and Springer doesn't. I make eye contact whether it's an obese woman, a person with AIDS, or a teenager with an addiction.

If you're talking to street people, you have to make eye contact to communicate with them. Psychologists are morally and ethically responsible to do this, in the media or not.

Lita: In what ways do you believe that we and our colleagues can use the media more effectively? In other words, how does a psychologist do a column? Or get into broadcasting? What are the how-tos? What are the differences in working between the two forms of the media? What are the "what not-to-dos"? Should we stay away from the media?

Dan: There are several ways we can use the media more effectively:

1. Know when to say no to the media. Sometimes if you say "No, thank you," you're striking a blow for the greater good [of mental health]. They want snap answers, and we shouldn't always give them.
2. I would like to see mental health professionals work together with the media to develop a new way of thinking. I would like to see mental health professionals initiate and do documentaries. We could get our own funding to do them. Until now, mental health psychologists have been dependent on the media to define what we say and how we say it. The media also select the topics that they deem relevant, and they define the structure around that topic. I would like to see psychologists create powerful documentaries around a whole variety of themes that could be educational and informative. For instance, I was at a conference in Washington, and I said I'd like to do a documentary on daily acts of heroism. As an example, take a 14-year-old girl going through puberty, maybe

she just got her period. She's got pimples on her face and thinks that all the kids hate her. There's nothing so rough as being isolated and lonely as a kid. Nevertheless, she puts both feet on the floor in the morning when she gets out of bed, makes herself up as pretty as she can, and despite her fear, anger, and insecurity, marches to school that day, performs, and then comes home. That's an act of heroism. And that doesn't get acknowledged.

There are lots of stories like that to make into documentaries. And a million variations. That's one thing we could do. We don't have to sit back and wait for someone to ask us our opinion.

3. Remember our responsibility: to inform and to educate, not to sell. When a psychologist calls me with an idea, I can tell immediately if they're trying to be self-promoting or have another marketing agenda. Remember, if you don't like the idea of the media manipulating you, you shouldn't manipulate the media.

4. The other thing when dealing with the media is to remember what we learned in graduate school. We need to speak so that the audience can understand us. On the other hand, don't be too simplistic and give answers that just don't exist. Too many mental health professionals are oversimplifying and giving formulas. I believe this is a disservice to the overall population and to ourselves.

Lita: Are there some differences that you find in working with the radio and writing the column?

Dan: Me, personally, yes, as a host and as a writer, I can write about whatever I want to write about and I don't feel as accountable. That is, it is not a team decision. I don't feel surrounded by a station manager, and so on, but the column is also much harder than the radio show.

Lita: You have a time limit on the radio show, with time out for announcements, public service commercials. . . . I assume you have a word limit on the column. . . .

Dan: Yes, roughly 800 to 1,100 words.

Lita: That's quite respectable. You get a lot across because you're very focused. . . . You have to be. I guess it would be easier to be diverted on the radio show.

Dan: Do you mean in terms of subject matter?

Lita: Yes, your guest may go off on a tangent.

Dan: Surprisingly, one of the most difficult things for me to do on the radio is really to attend to what my guest is saying in response to my questions. That is because I'm juggling so many balls at the same time. While my guest is speaking, I am going through my interview; at the same time, I'm looking to see whether there are calls, and I'm reading on the monitor what they are calling about, and I'm also focused on the clock to see when we have to take a break. Can I squeeze a caller in before the break? Is the show moving along quickly enough or too slowly? Yes, and all of that while I'm trying to listen to the content of what the guest is saying.

Lita: That's a talent! And I think that needs to be included because most of our colleagues are not juggling on a radio show, nor are they aware of the need for it on the host's part.

Lita: Other than the documentaries, are there other roles that mental health professionals have not yet explored? I'm starting to see articles on computer dependency, like overinvolvement with the Internet. For example, should we be dealing with the Internet/World Wide Web as a medium? Are there ways in which psychologists can help avoid such dependency or other negative effects of being on-line?

Dan: The American Psychological Association (APA) has dealt with Internet dependency somewhat. On the other hand, psychologists are doing psychotherapy on the Internet. It's almost like treating an alcoholic at a bar. It troubles me deeply. It's diminished humanity, it's diminished eye contact, and it's increased alienation. It just makes the question more confusing about "What does it mean to be human?" "What does it mean to be in a relationship?"

Like any other addiction, becoming overinvolved with chat rooms, video games, and various web sites fills a need that is not being satisfied in some healthier way. There is a lack of eye contact and a lack of human contact on the Internet. They diminish the chances for eye contact; for giving a person dignity. There is nothing more healing than that process. When I say to a caller, "Tell me your story," that person has the dignity of being recognized as someone worth listening to.

[Note: It was this eye contact that Devlin (1997) focused on in reporting on a talk that Gottlieb gave at a luncheon in Allentown, PA.]

In response to your original question, though, sure, there is much we can do. After all, psychologists should be about understanding and promoting mental health in the community. In that context, we should be more involved in politics and school boards. We could be more involved in community activism and even use our dispute-mediation skills in our own community.

Lita: In what ways do you think that the media can use us effectively?

Dan: We have to teach them how to use us. I think psychologists should be writing more op-ed pieces; they ought to be writing magazine articles.

Lita: Could psychologists possibly have positive impact, via the media, on some of our quandaries and problems, such as excessive violence shown in films and on TV and its effects on some children and adults? Emotional as well as physical abuse? Racial, religious, and ethnic prejudice and discrimination? Preparing children to make thoughtful choices? Reducing the prolonged postdivorce battles that harm the children as well as the adults? Transmitting information to reduce incidents such as the several neonaticides by young unwed women reported just in the New York–Washington corridor in the past few years? How can we help?

Dan: We can have impact through the documentaries I mentioned. These can teach parents and others. I'd like to do it in more interesting and different ways. We can get up there, and we can quote incidents and prevalence of spouse abuse; we can cite therapeutic interventions, and we can give phone numbers for resources. All of that's fine. But that comes up when an "OJ" hits the media. I would like to see us, if we did a documentary, do it in a way where we can teach spontaneously. The other thing is that we can think in terms of media so that, say, spouse abuse, can trigger an article or an op-ed piece.

I would love, if as a result of something that was reported in the media, a psychologist called me to say "Look what happened! I happen to be an expert on juvenile violence (for example), and I would like to talk with you about it." I would jump on that in a minute! I need my colleagues watching the media to see what's going on and being willing to address the problems with ideas. That's what I mean about focusing not on the self, but on ideas. Call me about Saddam Hussein. Or trauma.

Lita: Even if we do good documentaries, and they're on a major network instead of PBS, some people may watch, but maybe those to whom we're really aiming this would see *documentary* and watch *Rangers From Outer Space*, or something like that.

Dan: Yes, that is a problem. We'd have to find a name other than *documentary*. Some advertising person would be able to do that.

Psychologists can call program hosts to address topics of the day or volunteer to write for the papers. We need to become proactive.

Lita: Thank you, Dan.

Dan: Thank you! I didn't realize I had so many thoughts about these matters.

Speaking with Dan Gottlieb as interviewer or interviewee, and I have done both, is always a learning experience. In the talk printed here, I learned about him in terms of his media experience and his media approach. It was the latter, what he calls "eye contact," that was impressive for its simplicity and honesty, not to mention its rarity. That Dan conveys empathy in his writing and on the radio is well known in the Philadelphia area. He mentioned in our interview the significant breakthrough for him, as well as for his audience, in revealing himself on the air as a quadriplegic. Going back in the archives of the *Philadelphia Inquirer* before his first formal "On Healing" column, I found a printed article that he had written in response to a woman who had been in a car accident and who was having great difficulty living with the aftermath (Gottlieb, 1992). The sensitivity with which he responded, granted in part out of his own experience, is the essence of what he sees missing in some of the popular media "pop psychology" figures.

> Part of what makes pain worse—and this applies to any kind of pain—is the feeling of isolation we experience. We live in a world where near perfection is perceived as the ideal and anything less is shameful. . . . Nothing creates a sense of isolation more powerfully than when we are embarrassed about who we are or what we feel. (Gottlieb, 1992, p. F3)

This description of the sense of embarrassment and isolation is equally applicable to the adolescent girl he described as a candidate for a heroism award. Dan is interested not only in helping others to heal but also in finding ways in which psychologists can use the media constructively, rather than being used by the media. This may well be an appropriate mission for Division 46, Media Psychology, of APA.

References

DeAngelis, T. (1997, August). "Shock radio" is chasing away psychologists: In the era of "Dr. Laura," some psychologists opt out of radio programs. *APA Monitor, 28*(8), 10.

Devlin, F. (1997, March 20). Eye contact can change lives: Psychotherapist tells awards audience how to see beyond infirmities. *Allentown (PA) Morning Call*, p. B3.

Gottlieb, D. (1992, September 28). How a serious injury damages the body and soul. *Philadelphia Inquirer*, p. F3.

Sifford, D. (1982, November 25). Many find that they remember the story of an accident victim. *Philadelphia Inquirer*, p. E4.

Wylie, M. S. (1997, Sept./Oct.). America's therapist? Loving and loathing Dr. Laura. *Networker* (family therapy), pp. 11–12, 14.

Appendix

Sample Column Titles by Dan Gottlieb

6/21/93	"If a Child's Motivation Wanes, It's Essential to Root Out the Cause"
7/19/93	"A Husband's Expectations About Retired Life Clash With His Wife's"
8/2/93	"To Forgive Parents, Son of an Abusive Father Must Relinquish Anger"
2/6/95	"Woman's Sense of Emptiness Strikes a Responsive Chord in Others" [Written in response to a "flood of letters" about his column of 1/2/1995.]
3/17/97	"Parents Need to Know Signs of Emotional Disorders in Children"
6/2/97	"An Open Letter to Dad on Trauma and How Families Recover From It"
8/4/97	"Wrestling in Daily Life With Concepts of Death and Immortality"
10/6/97	"What Parents Can Do to Help Stem a Rising Tide of Juvenile Violence"
10/20/97	"The Toll of Domestic Abuse, and How Clergy Can Intervene"
11/3/97	"State Agency Isn't Blind, It Just Needs to Look"
11/17/97	"Mourning a Pet May Signify Deeper Distress"
12/15/97	"How to Find a Good Therapist Who Is Close to Your Home"
1/12/98	"Harsh Punishment Is Not a Wise Course When a Teen Son Is Drinking"
1/19/98	"A Death Prompts Reflections on Failure of So Many to Truly Connect"
2/2/98	"A Volunteer Finds a Colleague Troublesome"
2/16/98	"Eating Disorders in Girls Appear to Be Symbolic of a Greater Hunger"
4/6/98	"Her Shame-Filled Depression Has Roots in Early Sibling Sexual Abuse"

4

Using the Media to Promote Positive Images of Couples: A Multilevel Approach

Peter L. Sheras and Phyllis R. Koch-Sheras

Everywhere we look in the media today, we see evidence of psychology. Topics of psychological interest appear regularly on newscasts, on talk shows, in sitcoms, and in movies. That is the good news. The bad news is that often it is not professional psychologists who are teaching the public about these important topics, but rather Hollywood writers or talk show hosts functioning as "therapists without training" for the public, presenting scenarios and psychological conclusions that are sometimes incorrect or even harmful to viewers. There are ways, however, that we as psychologists can use this increasing interest in our field to positively influence attitudes and behaviors. In the case of our own work about couples, we describe here our attempts to do just that.

With the divorce rate at 50% and holding, the prevailing notion about relationships these days is that being part of a couple is a constant struggle and a no-win situation over the long haul. Even those couples who do stay married for many years tend to report decreasing levels of satisfaction the longer they are married. In addition, with the advent of dual-career couples, the continuing myth of the superwoman, increasing economic instability, and residential mobility, pressures on the concept of "the healthy couple" as a gratifying entity have intensified. The expectation for many people has been that being in a couple long-term is not much fun. Our commitment is to use the current interest in psychological issues in the media to demonstrate that satisfaction can be the hallmark of a stable relationship.

We describe here the steps we have taken to develop a multilevel media approach to promote a positive public perception about couples. People are exposed to the media in many ways. To impact the public, therefore, it seems necessary to address this issue through many different media. Although we have focused on the area of couples, you can apply the methods presented here to other areas of psychology as well.

Developing a Plan

A comprehensive strategy is required to develop a multilevel approach. Think of it as developing a "battle plan," with a variety of campaigns aimed in several directions to achieve the overall mission. Rather than just setting a goal, conceive of it as realizing a vision of what you want to accomplish— the way you would like the world to be.

Having a shared vision has been important for our own work. To impact large numbers of couples, we generated a coordinated effort for contacting professionals and reaching the public. Putting our idea for "a world of lasting and meaningful couple relationships" into words helped keep us on track. Coming from such a perspective, we could see a variety of available media outlets as opportunities to express our commitment to couples in an organized way.

Once we had created a statement that inspired us to take action, we stated it in understandable language as sound bite. The one we came up with was "Join the campaign for Couple Power." It encompassed all aspects of our endeavor and spoke directly to the public. To protect this product, we decided to obtain a trademark for our particular wording. This was a rather expensive process involving an extensive national and international search and legal documentation. We now use the trademark symbol with Couple Power in all our brochures and printed materials. It reminds us of our commitment to our vision.

We then developed a three-part media plan that included media presentations, products for training, and strategies for implementation. This gave us a structure to follow and a way to mark our progress. We describe below how we are carrying out this plan.

Using a Variety of Media

A comprehensive approach to changing couples' behavior included the use of varied media. If we ignored any of these aspects, we stood to miss a large part of our potential audience. We saw the need to access a wide range of media outlets, including television, radio, print, syndication, Internet, CD-ROMs, and training tapes. Our suggestions for using each of these are described below. We focus on those areas in which we have had the most personal experience.

Television

In working with television or radio, there is the possibility of appearing on someone else's show or producing your own program. Although the notion of putting together your own show may sound daunting, it may not be as difficult as you think.

Appearing on others' shows. We were often asked to be interviewed on a news or feature program on the topic of couples or in some other area. Generally, producers got our name through our publisher or through the American Psychological Association (APA) Media Referral Service. Given our commitment to couples, we always tried to include, whenever feasible, some information in that area. Thus, if Phyllis was being interviewed about dreams, she was sure to include something about how sharing dreams, both night dreams and waking visions, could enhance a couple relationship. We would also bring in the notion of couple by sometimes suggesting that the two of us appear together. That is what happened, for example, when Phyllis was invited to be interviewed about dreams on a television show in a nearby city. When the producers brought up the possibility of including an additional expert, they agreed to Phyllis's suggestion of having Peter appear with her. Including the couple in the interview led to an interesting show that enabled us to cover both the areas of dreams and couple relationships.

In addition to one-shot interviews, we also became part of a television series. We did this through our relationship with a small independent producer. We told him of our commitment to couples work, and we laid the groundwork for several possible projects with him on this subject. When an opportunity arose for him to produce a series of programs on psychological topics for a national cable network, he thought that a couple perspective from professionals would be a good addition. We helped him generate a number of appropriate topics, such as grief, death, loneliness, and guilt, and we appeared in 14 of the shows. The program was broadcast twice a week in major cities around the country and has continued in reruns for several years. It was an interesting and enjoyable project, and we even received a small honorarium for each show. All of this came out of keeping our commitment to couples out in front and sharing it on a continual basis with people who had connections to the media. We are still in conversation with this producer about other possible projects that he might produce related to the area of couples.

Producing our own show. With the encouragement of colleagues and friends, we decided to produce our own show about couples. Because the area of production was new to us, we hired a consultant from a local university to help us put the show together. Our plan was to submit it to some networks and/or present it on our local public-access television channel. We also had the assistance of some interested psychology graduate students who helped us brainstorm about the content of the show.

What we created was a program presenting positive models of couples living their lives and solving their everyday problems. The show, *The Couple Power Half Hour*, cohosted by us, was a combination of a talk show, general advice program, and interview show. It opened with a musical slide presentation of couples by a local portrait photographer. We then conducted a spontaneous studio interview with a successful couple. At this point, we entertained questions from a live audience. When there was no live audience, we included a set of "people-on-the-street" interviews, asking such questions as "Are you difficult to live with?" The show closed with our comments about current movies or news events related to couples. The topic for the next show was presented, and we faded to more music and slides.

The show was shown several times on our local public-access television channel, which provided free studio and broadcast time as well as production equipment. To produce more shows, Peter enrolled in the training program provided by the local cable company. It provided instruction in the production of noncommercial programs of community interest. The crew for the next show consisted of other trainees. We taped the program in the public-access television studio, and it was aired several times during the next month. The local newspaper did an interview with us about the show, and it received a very positive response from the community.

Producing our own show was enjoyable and very rewarding, but it took a lot of time and effort. A more efficient way to produce this kind of program might be through an independent producer, a local television station, or a cable network. The show we designed for this purpose was called *The Couple Power Hour*. Proposed topics for that show included "Beginnings: Great stories about getting together," "Finding a good partner: Where to look and what to look for," and "Great arguments: Good, bad, ugly?"

Getting on television may not be as difficult as you imagine. Giving a cold call to your local TV station or a reporter is a good start.

Radio

We found a number of ways to use radio to educate the public on psychological issues. It was generally easier to pursue than television, as it was often more accessible locally and nationally through telephone hookup.

One-shot interviews. A single, one-shot interview is the most common type of radio appearance. We have often spoken on radio talk shows in other cities. This can be done by telephone connection, even the call-in segments. These can be relatively simple to arrange at your home or office, and a program may reach a wide audience. Radio talk shows are particularly interested in you if you have something timely to share—a hot topic in the news or a new book, for example. If you have a book, these appearances can be arranged through your publisher. If you are not satisfied with the results, consider hiring an independent publicist to arrange interviews for you.

If you do not have a publisher or publicist, you can contact local radio stations yourself and let them know what you are willing and able to talk about. Ask to talk to either the program manager or the host of a health program, news, or human-interest show. Sometimes someone from a local station will have heard about you and will call on their own. This occurred for us with a local station that asked us to be on a 2-hour call-in show about relationships. The interview was no problem, but there were relatively few call-ins. It seems that people are reluctant to call in about personal issues in their relationships on a local station, particularly if it is in a small town such as ours. (We did talk during the show with the host about his own relationship with his girlfriend, and he greatly appreciated the help.)

With another station, we contacted the director of a free clinic who hosted a weekly interview show on topics related to health issues. We told her about our work with couples, and she arranged for us to be interviewed on her half-hour show. At the time that our *Couple Power Hour* television show was about to air, we also did an interview on a weekly radio news show. The request for that interview came out of a newspaper article done about the show. This illustrates how a media opportunity in one medium can lead to one in another. A one-shot interview can also lead to a long-term arrangement with a radio station. Though many of these overtures may not succeed, do not be discouraged, and keep exploring possible contacts.

Ongoing programming. Once you have your foot in the door at a particular radio station, you can capitalize on your contacts there to create opportunities for some long-term programming, either on someone else's show or for your own radio show. It may take several tries, but if you persist, you are likely to find the right person at the right time. That was our experience with our local talk radio station. After a few appearances on the station, we suggested to the host of the daily community interview program that we appear as regulars on the show. Hosts of such shows often want the same guests for particular topics so that they do not have to set up new interviews every week. After a few months, the host called and said they had decided to use a model for regular alternating segments on various subjects and that they would like to have us do one of the segments on the topic of couples. We began to appear on the show live in the studio once or twice a month for a 7–8-minute interview segment. For each show, we would talk to the host the day before to confirm the topic and title of the segment for that week. Some of the titles included "Romance and Reality," "Creating a Couple Vision," "Valentine's Day—Not Just a Box of Chocolates," "Infidelity—The Fantasy and the Reality," and "Dealing With Stress About the Holidays as a Couple." For each show, we created three main points and three tips for the listeners. That structure allowed us to be prepared and spontaneous at the same time.

Print

The aspect of the media that we have spent perhaps the most time with is in the area of print, both giving interviews and writing our own material. Writing can be difficult work and takes a lot of concentration, but we have found it to be extremely rewarding both personally and professionally. Whatever you publish can lend credibility to your professional work.

General publications.

Books. It is important in writing for a trade book audience to keep the writing simple and lively, avoiding psychological jargon or turgid language. This can be particularly difficult with certain topics, especially if the concepts are not already a part of commonly used language. We found that to be the case when writing about the ontological aspects of being a couple. To keep ourselves on target, we hired a freelance writer who specialized in editing professional material. She could pick up more readily than we could, particularly in the early stages of our writing, the "fifty-cent words" and where we were getting bogged down in tone or phrasing. As time went on, it became easier to write for a lay audience and to enjoy doing it.

We wrote our first book together *The Dream Sourcebook Journal* (Koch-Sheras & Sheras, 1996) in collaboration with this editor, and she also edited some chapters in our later book, *The Dream Sharing Sourcebook: A Practical Guide to Enhancing Your Personal Relationships* (Koch-Sheras & Sheras, 1998). This second book grew out of material in the first one related to couples working together on their dreams. The publisher particularly liked that part of the first book and asked us to submit a book proposal on the topic of dreams and relationships. Although that was not exactly the couples book we were planning, it seemed like a good move in that direction. It turned out to be a wonderful opportunity to elaborate fully on the uses of dreams in relationships, through both sleeping and waking visions, and to advance our ideas about relationships in the media.

We are always committed to producing new publications about our work with couples. To accomplish this, it may be useful to find a literary agent to get a book contract. Once you have a contract, it is wise to go over it with an attorney before signing. Do not be afraid to ask colleagues for help.

Particularly in popular areas of publication such as couples and relationships, the competition can be intense. Once you have a publisher, you can often continue to produce further work with that same company. We obtained a publisher in one case when we were asked to do a professional edit of someone's book. During that project, the idea for a book emerged and was ultimately accepted for publication. That contract led to the next two books mentioned above. It works to just keep your vision out in front and stick with it.

Magazines. Trade magazines are a popular source of media opportunities. Every month, these magazines need to fill their pages with interesting material, and there are countless freelance and magazine staff writers out there looking for quotes from experts, frequently on the topic of relationships. They usually reached us through APA or our university media referral service. When we told writers that we could be interviewed as a professional couple, they were almost always receptive to getting a male–female perspective.

In addition to granting interviews, you might want to write and submit an article of your own. The place to start is to send a query letter to the magazines that best fit your topic. (The query should briefly summarize the rationale for and give the content of your proposed article and provide biographical information.) Phyllis sent out a few query letters on the topic of "family dreamwork" several years ago, and she was given a contract for the article by a popular women's magazine. The magazine paid full fee for the article, whether they printed it or not.

Another possibility in the area of magazines is to propose doing a regular column in your area of expertise that could be of interest to that publication's readership. Sometimes magazines have regular staff to perform that function, but they may be open to the idea. We approached our regional monthly magazine about doing a regular column about couples. They did not have space for it in their current plans for the year, but may be open to it in the future.

Newspapers. Your local newspaper is a readily available avenue for sharing information on psychological topics of current interest. Through op-ed pieces, letters to the editor, or perhaps even a regular column, it is possible to bring some important information to the public's attention. We recently wrote some letters to the editor of our local newspaper about political issues related to couples and families. We acknowledged the contributions of particular political leaders to the welfare of families. Several people commented to us about the letters, including some who called asking for therapy appointments. Thus, you can see that getting your name in print is good exposure for promoting your ideas as well as your business.

Professional publications. It is important to have concrete research or scholarly underpinnings for what we do in the popular media. That is where professional books, chapters, and journal articles come in. It may be easier to start small and work up, creating the groundwork for a book with an article or chapter in an edited book. That is what we did when we approached a colleague who edited a psychology series. We used material from our couples therapy training workshops to put together a chapter for a professional series (Sheras & Koch-Sheras, 1998). Writing a chapter can lead to requests by others interested in publishing your work.

The only drawback to having many irons in the fire in the media is that they may all catch on at the same time. If they do, you can spread out your commitments and negotiate contract deadlines. What is crucial is to keep the "big picture" and your vision in front of you at all times.

Syndication

Syndication is the process whereby your articles or shows are given to more than a single media outlet, to other stations or publications. It might mean that a show done once could be rebroadcast later in other markets or that your media piece might appear in more than one market at the same time. At the level of our work, and for most psychologists trying to establish a media presence, however, syndication is not the first step. For us, it has been a process of making sure that our work is recorded and that we keep track of articles, radio and television shows, and interviews. We try to make sure to have audio- or videotapes of what we do. Periodically, we edit together samples of our work as a "demo," or illustration tape, which we can send to those who may be interested in working with us.

The Internet or Other Electronic Media

Computer media technology is growing incredibly fast. A good, well-functioning web site can prove to be a boon for providing information to the public and advertising books or workshops. Depending on your goals, time, and ambition, an interactive site can allow you to refer people to other web sites for information and can also be used to communicate directly with those who contact your site. It is possible to sell products through this medium and even count the number of inquiries, or "hits," to your web page. If you are not well versed in how to do this, the services of a web master can be obtained. A deluxe web site with interactive elements can be costly and time-consuming but, in the long run, can give you a great deal of exposure. Again, you may want to consult an attorney regarding the protection of your intellectual property rights. Our Couple Power web page is still under construction. It will at least provide information about books, articles, and workshops but may be expanded to become more interactive to answer questions.

Electronic mail is another method for communicating with a wider audience. We have been using our E-mail address to obtain comments from practitioners we have trained in workshops. It allows us to hear what has been learned and offer return comments and support. It is also a sort of "living" feedback that aids us in updating our work and keeping our vision current.

In addition to using on-line resources, information in new electronic formats is continually evolving. Interactive CD-ROMs can be produced to provide training or publicity. The technology and production costs in electronic media are continually decreasing in price. We have not yet embarked on production of this level of material, but it is likely to be part of any significant attempt to harness the media to make a point in the future.

Marketing and Training Materials

Workshops for professionals and the general public are useful ways of publicizing your vision, and you will need to have materials to support these endeavors. The major first step for us was to produce a brochure about our work. Once we had a design that we liked, we could change it slightly depending on the target audience. With advances in desktop publishing and the easy accessibility to small printers that can lay out brochures on the computer, finding and working with a designer were not very difficult. We produced a number of brochures and fliers that make suitable mailers, handouts, and handbills. These tools can briefly state your vision, publicize your work, and express your creativity at the same time. In addition to individual biographies, our Couple Power brochure includes a biography of us as a couple, because we wanted to make the point that a couple is more than just the sum of two individuals. A good professional photo or graphic is also helpful. We sometimes included a tear-off sheet, order blank, or reply card, so that we could be reached and expand our mailing list.

You may want to put your marketing information together in a media kit that includes all of the above plus references, interview questions, and so forth; or you might create a video or audio resume of clips of your various media presentations. These materials are very useful to give to reporters or interviewers. They provide concise statements of who you are and what you do.

Use of training tapes, video manuals, and CD-ROMs can be a powerful component of a media plan. We noticed recently that our new vacuum cleaner came with not only an instruction manual but also a video that we could watch while figuring it out. This message of convenience is an important one. Until your ideas are established, they must be accessible and convenient. For instance, appearances on radio during drive time or TV during leisure time may make your ideas easy to hear.

Developing Contacts

Perhaps the most important thing you have to do to use the media effectively in expressing your ideas is to get coverage. In most cases, you will need to seek out this coverage. We found that although we think that being in a healthy and satisfying relationship is newsworthy, most reporters and producers do not necessarily see that as news. Unless there is a cogent news item related to what you do, people will not come looking for you. The key, then, is to develop contacts. Once a contact has been made, it is important to use and expand that relationship. Below are some of the techniques we have used to gain greater acceptance for our notions of maintaining positive relationships. We were fortunate in that our topic was one that most reporters and producers would understand. They were mostly in relationships themselves and would like to improve them, or were in great relationships and want to brag about them. (On several occasions, we have helped a host or reporter resolve difficulties in their own relationship during the interview.)

Get Listed as an Expert

Reporters, hosts, and producers are constantly looking for experts to interview or use on shows and in articles. It is important to establish yourself. Professional associations such as APA have media referral services to respond to inquiries on a variety of subjects. Most major universities and companies have news offices whose job is to promote their professionals or faculty as experts to the media. Make sure they know you. Many have a form to complete. We listed our expertise as psychologists working with couples with the

APA Media Referral Service and our university news service. When there is a reporter who needs an expert in this area, we are called. These lists have given us interviews in major magazines for women and parents in the past few years. They also have yielded contacts for news reports as well as radio and television shows on topics related to marriage, adultery, couples therapy, domestic conflict, working with the opposite sex, dreams and relationships, and the like.

Offer Your Help

Expose yourself to the general public whenever possible. If you want to be known for your work, you have to give some of your time away. Plan to speak to your local Mental Health Association or support groups in your area. We occasionally advertise miniworkshops or lectures that are open to the public at no charge in the newspaper or on the radio. If there is a local reporter who has some interest in the topic of our presentation, we invite him or her to attend.

When contacted by a reporter, try to be helpful. Do not assume an adversarial relationship. The more cooperative you are, the more likely you will be called again. When a contact is made by telephone for an interview, we always ask the reporter to talk a little about the goal of his or her piece and the deadlines. When possible, we arrange a later time to talk after we have had the opportunity to prepare our sound bites and the three major points we would like to make. Whenever we can, we try to do our interviews as a couple. It provides a slightly different angle for the reporter, gives us the chance to play off each other, and demonstrates some of the major points we want to make about couples. Whether interviewed separately or together, we try to get our readers, viewers, and listeners to understand that a couple is an entity with its own personality; by being interviewed together, we can demonstrate this. By being friendly and cooperative, we have found that our discussions with reporters or producers often last considerably longer than planned. Look for openings to suggest additional ideas or even other experts.

Sometimes the most difficult decision to make during an interview is how much of your original material to share. Remember to look at your vision of what you are committed to accomplish. Is this sort of media exposure designed to educate the public, whet the appetite of consumers or potential clients, or get some name recognition for yourself? If you have books, articles, or workshops available, give a little content and then refer the audience to those.

Track Your Contacts

We keep track of all our media contacts. This is important for a number of reasons. Many times you may be interviewed well in advance of the publication or airing of the piece. For magazines, sometimes 8 months may lapse before an article is printed. Our contact form (see Appendix) helps us remember when to look for the piece. Whenever we speak with an interviewer, we always ask to see a copy of what has been produced. We may be promised a faxed copy of an article or a "dub" (a copy of a video- or audiotape) of a radio or television show. In actuality, the print pieces are rarely sent. Our contact forms help us remember when to look for these.

It is important to record on the contact form information about reporters, including their phone number for future reference. You may want to approach them at a later time to suggest a piece or follow up something you have done with them. Our contact form also includes a brief summary of the topic of the article and what we said. We leave a few lines to write each of the main points or sound bites we used. At the bottom is space for a numerical rating of how well we thought the interview went. We place these contact sheets in a loose-leaf binder to keep for future reference. It is interesting at the end of the year to review the contacts. This information can be used when "pitching" another interview or on a resume.

There Are No Small Contacts or Irrelevant Topics

Contacts with reporters, producers, hosts, or publishers are always important, not just when you want them to publicize your work immediately. These people may want to contact you later, have you work with them on a different topic, or use you as a resource. If you have a good media style on the page or on the air, you may be someone who is called on regularly. We have made contacts at parties, at ball games, and at radio and TV station open houses. Do not be shy. Introduce yourself and describe what you do. Share your interests and let people know that you are familiar with their work (if you are). Do not be too concerned if they don't want to focus on your specific topic. You may just need to get your foot in the door first. We have had a number of reporters come back to us later to talk about the couples' angle for stories they are working on. As mentioned earlier, we had a producer book us to do appearances as commentators on a show he was working on that needed some relationship perspective. Keep your contacts alive. Be back in touch with reporters regularly. Have a place in your media notebook to record ideas for future articles or shows. Also, get a list of radio and television stations in your area and the names of the program directors.

Develop a Relationship

Whenever you speak with a media contact, remember that you want to build a long-term relationship with that person. Treat him or her as a friend. These people, more than most others, can help you realize your vision. They are the doors to your wider exposure and the greater understanding of your ideas. We knew that we were succeeding in teaching reporters about the positive possibilities for couples when our interviewers started to talk with us about their own relationships. In many cases, we would chat with them about other work they were doing. In the case of many magazine writers, they are freelancers and may be developing ideas for future articles. After an interview on a particular topic, some writers have chosen to write more about the quality of our couple relationships than about the original topic.

In many cases, a good relationship with a reporter is a great resource. They may share your name with others. In one case, a television news magazine decided not to do a segment on our work but suggested it to another program at the station. Your skills as a psychologist in rapport building can be used here to listen to those who speak with you as you might listen to clients, carefully and with respect. Reporters will notice that you are cooperative and engaging and consider using you again. If you have done a good interview with someone, tell him or her directly that you would like to work together again.

Be Yourself

Above all, when dealing with the media, even though the situation may seem awkward, try to be yourself. Remember that everyone has the same goal in mind. Try to be relaxed and authoritative. The only exception may be some talk radio or tabloid television shows where emotional upset is their intention. Try to steer clear of these unless you are very aware of what you are doing. We have declined some opportunities because we considered them unethical. Producers in one case tried to convince us that revealing confidences of clients on television, with their permission, would not affect our subsequent therapeutic relationship with them. "Clients love this sort of thing," they said. We disagreed and declined to be involved under those conditions. We suggested using friends or acquaintances rather than client couples, but this option did not materialize.

One way to work on being natural and being yourself is to review interviews and tapes of your work. Show them to others for some hard criticism. The questions that we often ask each other after an appearance are, Did we act like ourselves? Did we seem relaxed and alive? Were we being clear? Above all, the best way to learn to maintain a relaxed demeanor is to practice. Do as many appearances or interviews as you possibly can. Experience is the best trainer in most cases. Do not be afraid if you look or sound a little stiff in the beginning. Much of this is anxiety. With repetition and familiarity comes the natural tendency to be yourself on the air or in print.

Impacting the Public

Our primary goal with working in the media was to promote our vision of Couple Power to the widest possible audience. It is our belief that the greatest effect of our attempts to change the paradigm of how most people think about relationships can be obtained by speaking and writing in as many public venues as possible. Our plan was to demonstrate, illustrate, and be a couple everywhere, making people aware that we were doing exactly that. Through radio, television, and print, we developed a regular presence in the minds of local and regional viewers as "that couple that speaks about Couple Power." We even had a brief conversation with a congressman friend of ours about the idea of having a couple run for public office, not to share the job, but to do it as a couple, stressing the power of relationship in public life.

We know, as marital therapists, that it is very difficult to impact people before they need treatment. We see the media, however, as a way to educate the general public to recognize the power of their own relationship daily. In this way, we hope to raise our audience's awareness and make a few major points repeatedly.

Ongoing Support for Couples

We believe that relationships need regular and effective support. Despite our culture's tendency to support masculine notions of independence and individuality, we can see that interdependence and values that promote sharing are essential to having healthy and long-lasting relationships. These long-term relationships produce the kind of couples that are the bedrock of solid families and provide the most fertile soil for developing healthy and well-adjusted children. We are fond of saying that "a good couple is the source of a good family." By appearing frequently in the media with regular spots on radio and television, books, journal articles, and news pieces, we want to illustrate that people in healthy relationships can help one another and create a community of mutually supportive couples.

Media Personalities Become Extended Family

It has become clear to us is that Americans spend a great deal of time reading magazines, watching television, and listening to the radio. The characters in soap operas, news anchors, and talk show hosts are our constant companions, being with us more than many of our relatives and close friends. Although this can be worrisome, it is also a great opportunity. Because many people now look to sports figures or media idols as role models, it is possible to highlight the positive aspects of relationships in the media and point out how some of these idols are in good relationships. This thought gave us the idea, for instance, to develop a segment for our cable TV show reviewing popular movies for themes of couples and examining the relationships of common sitcom characters. We attempted to show that well-functioning couples and families could be interesting and newsworthy. At the same time, the presentation of these couples can leave powerful and memorable positive images.

Using the Media as a Daily "Practice"

Involvement with the media is a regular ritual for many modern Americans. Reading the editorials in the paper, watching a talk show, listening to the news while driving to work, or enjoying a personal growth book is a habit for most and is only slightly less than an obsession for others. If we want people to think more positively about their relationships, we have to make sure that positive examples and ideas about couples are regularly present in these media outlets.

Getting the message out about healthy, positive, and enjoyable relationships involves a commitment to involving the media broadly in whatever we do. Our ideas need to become commonplace in the minds of the public. Using the influence of the media is not just a way to market our workshops or sell our books. It is conceptually essential to influencing the minds and hearts of the audience, those we want to help.

Summary and Recommendations

Our odyssey through the world of media began with our vision to change the prevailing ideas people had about relationships. At first, we thought that being excellent marital therapists would make the greatest contribution to this change. We saw, however, that by the time couples came to see us, they already held a number of preconceptions about marriages or committed relationships that made it difficult to treat them. We concluded that the assumptions about being together already learned in our culture were driving people to be more dissatisfied, more demanding, and more individualistic. As many authors have noted (Bellah, Sullivan, & Tipton, 1985; Montouri & Conti, 1993; and Wuthrow, 1994), individuals have become more concerned with the identification and satisfaction of their personal needs than developing a sense of cooperation or community with others. Couples have lost sight of the fact that a good relationship might *not* require losing oneself or giving in all the time. We thought long and hard about what might change this predicament that was tearing at the fabric of our family structures. We saw that changing the public's thoughts and behaviors in relationships would require comprehensive action. We thought of it as a campaign. It required strategy, tactics, and commitment on our part.

Create a Vision

Like any campaign (e.g., an advertising campaign, a campaign during a war, a political campaign), we needed to develop a broad plan, one that spanned a number of years and could be waged on many fronts. The first step was to imagine what the world would be like for couples when we were successful. We looked into the future to see how we would know we were in this "new world." This was the process of creating a vision. We spoke often of what Couple Power would be like and began to live our own life that way. We sensed early on that our vision would only be powerful if others knew about it. Expressing it in the media to a wide audience was clearly our major strategy.

Make a Plan

We began to plan how we could develop our ideas and let people know about them. We saw that using many forms of media could express our vision to couples at all levels functioning. We began to strategize regularly about expressing ourselves publicly using radio, TV, and print media. Our morning often began with discussion of work we would do that week on our "campaign for positive relationships." We wrote down our ideas, timetables, deadlines, and goals.

Get Coaching

Soon we realized that our idea was too big and too important for us to do by ourselves. We needed help to implement our plan, accomplish our goals, and realize our vision. Support and, above all, coaching for us were essential. We started to ask more questions to people who were in successful couple relationships. We asked friends, graduate students in psychology, reporters, artists, photographers, producers, and most anyone we could find to tell us their ideas. Our strategy focused on gathering information in the public arena about relationships from lectures and workshops, magazines, talk shows, call-in programs, and the like. The media became a two-way street, a method to speak to others and a way to hear from them. With some of our friends, we began coaching and being coached by other committed couples as well as having successful relationships. Weekly calls with other couples over the past 8 years have helped us to keep on track, keeping our relationship and our vision for the future in focus.

Measure the Results

How did we do? As we have been summarizing our work, we have noticed that much has been accomplished. Our task is large, and the specific results are difficult to measure. We notice increasing acceptance of our work, more popularity in local media, and more groups coming to us for workshops and advice. In a project of this magnitude, we need to be patient about immediate impact. It will take time. Meanwhile, we will continue to live our life in the kind of marriage we love and use the media to help us publicize our campaign for positive relationships. We are committed to create a cultural drift toward lasting and meaningful couple relationships throughout the world.

References

Bellah, R. N., Sullivan, W. M., & Tipton, S. M. (1985). *Habits of the heart: Individualism and community in American life*. Los Angeles: University of California Press.

Koch-Sheras, P. R., & Sheras, P. L. (1996). *The dream sourcebook journal*. Los Angeles: Lowell House.

Koch-Sheras, P. R., & Sheras, P. L. (1998). *The dream sharing sourcebook: A practical guide to enhancing your personal relationships*. Los Angeles: Lowell House.

Montouri, A., & Conti, I. (1993). *From power to partnership: Creating the future of love, work and community*. San Francisco: Harper San Francisco.

Sheras, P. L., & Koch-Sheras, P. R. (1998). New frontiers in treating couples. In L. VandeCreek, S. Knapp, & T. Jackson (Eds.), *Innovations in clinical practice* (Vol. 16, pp. 399–418). Sarasota, FL: Professional Resource Press.

Wuthrow, R. (1994). *Sharing the journey*. New York: Free Press.

APPENDIX

MEDIA CONTACT FORM

General Topic: _____

Air/PublicationDate: _____

Type of Media: ☐ TV   ☐ Radio   ☐ Print

Contact Date/s: _____

Publication/Program: _____

Interviewer/Author: _____

Producer/Editor: _____   Phone: _____

Address: _____

Angle: _____

Others Interviewed: _____

Points Prepared:
1.
2.
3.

Additional Points Made:
1.
2.
3.

Performance Rating (✓):

	Excellent	Very Good	Good	Fair	Poor
Content					
Style					
Comfort Level					
Credibility					
Professionalism					
Appearance					
Overall					

Was the relationship with the host/interviewer (circle)?

HOSTILE   CONFRONTATIONAL   DIRECT   COOPERATIVE   SUPPORTIVE

Follow-Up Planned:

Future Topics for this Source:

II

Media Portrayals
of Different Groups
Over Time

Part I ends looking at couples, and Part II begins focusing on the same theme. In this case, the couples are choosing a movie to watch (in a cinema), and Rosalie Greenfield Matzkin tries to find out who makes the choice and why. What can this information tell us about marital harmony and disharmony? Are there differences between dating couples and married couples?

It is a natural progression from couples to families, and Patricia Pitta provides a "then and now" view of the family myths presented on television over the past half-century as they moved from idealization to greater reality. Indeed, there were reports in mid-1998 that Ozzie and Harriet (Nelson) and their children did not have as idyllic a family life as was portrayed in their television program a few decades ago. Another myth blown to bits! Pitta also mentions the problems of stereotyping by gender, race, and age in these family-centered programs.

Rochelle Balter, who works with the physically challenged, examines the ways in which films and television show people with visual, hearing, orthopedic, and other physical challenges. How often have films or television portrayed those with challenges? How accurate and how empathetic are these views? Have there been changes since the passage of the Americans With Disabilities Act? Some of the more influential, and positive, films have been Charlie Chaplin's *City Lights* (1930), *Best Years of Our Lives* (1946), *Johnny Belinda* (1948), *The Miracle Worker* (1962), and *Elephant Man* (1980) (Michal-Smith, 1987). On the other hand, Balter also shows ways in which the portrayal has been weak or damaging. Perhaps there is a role here for knowledgeable psychologists to serve as consultants, she suggests, along with members of the physically challenged community.

The final chapter, by Lita Linzer Schwartz and Rosalie Greenfield Matzkin, focuses on the media and youth violence. Not all youths are violent, and not all violent youths are the product of hyped-up media presentations, but there are connections—and some antidotes. There are also connections between violent families and violent youths (Jouriles et al., 1998), and between the model (often graphically shown on television) of the short tempers of too many adults and the similar almost reflex behavior of too many young people: interpersonal incivility that has become all too familiar. The magnitude of the problem of violent youths and the contributions of the media to it provide a worthy mission for this division to assume as a particular responsibility for reduction.

Have you watched a television program, read an article, or heard a broadcaster make generalizations about a group and thought about how many people were influenced by the words or behaviors of that group? At least one introductory text provides perspectives for students in this realm (Dines & Humez, 1995). Comments in a media review similarly point out the contribution that articles on adoption in popular print media make to the thinking of pregnant teens about this option (Reese, 1997).

As practitioners, we have to be conscious of the ways in which the media portray different groups today and how they have done it in the past. It is our hope that these chapters will make readers even more cognizant of how psychology is used by the media for its own, or its advertisers', purposes. More important, perhaps, is the illumination of the many themes presented here that indicate how important it is for psychologists to contribute to the media in a positive and constructive way. Psychologists' words *do* make a difference!

References

Dines, G., & Humez, J. M. (1995). *Gender, race, and class in media*. Thousand Oaks, CA: Sage.

Jouriles, E. N., McDonald, R., Norwood, W. D., Ware, H. S., Spiller, L. C., & Swank, P. R. (1998). Knives, guns, and interparent violence: Relations with child behavior problems. *Journal of Family Psychology, 12,* 178–194.

Michal-Smith, H. (1987). Presidential address 1987: Hollywood's portrayal of disability. *Mental Retardation, 25,* 259–266.

Reese, C. O. (1997). Adoption in the media. *Adoption Quarterly, 1*(1), 85–91.

Take Me Out to a Movie!

Rosalie Greenfield Matzkin

When I was 20, I met a girl in Rome. We were standing by the Spanish Steps waiting for the American Express office to open. Like me, she was a visiting student, and she seemed quite pleasant. We went to a movie together. Unfortunately, she liked the movie, and I didn't. Neither of us could forgive the other's bad taste, and the relationship quickly soured. It's happened to me a few times since. I like to talk about movies, and despite hating most of them, I keep going in the hope that this time it'll be an elevating experience. But I'm barely capable of suspending disbelief long enough. It's not that I'm an intellectual. I couldn't tell you what film noir is and don't know one director from another. But I do know this: Movies are a sticky subject, and they can test the mettle of a relationship. They are to my generation what politics and religion were to previous ones. Shallow? Stupid? Perhaps, but no less true. We take on movies as a mask of our own identity, so disagreement becomes a very personal matter. (Pitock, 1997, p. E7)

Unlike the op-ed writer above, most people probably do not "hate" most movies they see. Nor is it likely that many romances have been cut off because of a single movie-related dispute. Nonetheless, for certain kinds of moviegoers, movie partnering (the "who" of moviegoing) can be as significant a part of the experience as the "when," "where," and "what" of the movies they see. Indeed, I have heard enough stories and been in enough situations where movie engagements and/or discussions were fraught with controversy to conclude that going to the movies and movie talk can be controversial, can, in fact, challenge the equilibrium of people's interactions, at least temporarily. In contrast to other mass media encounters, the movie experience seems to intrude more deeply into the complicated elements of the human psyche and human heart. "Every film is a Rorschach Test," a former professor of mine suggested, using that thesis as the title of his critical textbook on elements of film aesthetics. In it he observed that "because of our backgrounds, our experiences, we all react differently to films, and to all artistic experiences" (Forsdale, 1976, Mini-Dialog 1). The sense of validation when we feel agreement can bring us closer to others with whom we share an experience. Conversely, a sense of its lack can provoke a gulf when we disagree, because our views are always filtered through our own personal and highly selective perceptual screens (Forsdale, 1976, Mini-Dialog 1).

Moviegoing: A Social Phenomenon

Clearly, going to the movies is a social experience. Most people do not go alone, they go with someone. Moreover, movie talk is quite common in this mass media drenched era.

> The pervasiveness of the influences of movies and movie conventions on our day to day lived-worlds is visible in the smallest details of urban existence: movie ads, movie lines, movie sweatshirts, movie critic television shows. One hears movie song themes, allusions to movies and performers even in encounters with other media, including books; not simply among children and teenagers, but among adults as well. (Matzkin, 1985, p. 4)

A tally of the personals in *Philadelphia City Paper*, a local weekly newspaper, and an issue of *Philadelphia Magazine*, a monthly magazine, indicated that single people seeking companions, romance, and courtship, often identify themselves as moviegoers and seek others who enjoy the film experience as well (see Exhibit 1).

One can hardly walk through a restaurant, or up to a water cooler, sit in a doctor's office or hair salon, without picking up snatches of movie conversation, or without overhearing some reference to the mass media scene and to current cinematic titles. Film talk and encounters seem, in certain adult circles larger than my own, full of complexities. Such encounters can be very intense; can, in fact, be provocative.

Conventions of Moviegoing: A Very Brief History

We tend to take our moviegoings and viewings rather for granted these days. While motion pictures have been around for over 100 years now, the uses, conventions, and makeup

---

Exhibit 1

Results from Moviegoing Tallies in Philadelphia Magazine *and the* Philadelphia City Paper

---

1. *Philadelphia Magazine*: (Personals, 1998a, pp. 171–174)
   Total = 8 who indicate movies or moviegoing as a leisure time activity.
2. *Philadelphia City Paper*: (Personals, 1998b, pp. 102–103)
   Women seeking men = 19
   Double-dating = 1
   Men seeking women = 22
   Men seeking men = 2
   Women seeking women = 1
3. Reviewing another week's worth of personal ads in August of 1998 produced findings that were consistent with those in May.

of audiences have been through historic shifts and mutations through the decades. During its earliest days and throughout the silent movie era ending in the late 1920s, the working poor and immigrants were Hollywood's first and most loyal audiences. Especially for those enraptured audiences who had not yet learned English, the subtle and carefully shaded acting techniques perfected by the end of the silent screen era, and further enhanced by richly impressionistic live musical accompaniment, communicated volumes. The advent of talkies propelled the middle classes as well as the "leisure classes" into becoming fans. By the end of the 1920s, audiences were no longer homogeneous; everyone went out to the movies. During the height of the Great Depression (1929–1939), 90 million people—almost the entire nation—filled the movie palaces of America every week. In those days, movie program bills offered continuous showings, including two full-length features, at least one short, a travel film or newsreel, and a cartoon, as well as several coming attractions. Most viewers did not pay much attention to whether a film was directed by Frank Capra, Preston Sturges, or John Ford. They did go to see Mary Pickford, Douglas Fairbanks, or Gary Cooper. For many, the movie palace was a place to go to hold hands and be alone in the dark, or to escape into another more exotic world. Or, because of the Hays Code (the industrywide set of regulations and taboos on sexual content, aspects of violence, and other controversial subject matter, which operated under Hollywood's production system), movies were safe enough, as well as inexpensive enough, so that parents could bring the children along. It was, after all, grand simply getting out of the house.

After the emergence of television, motion picture production declined, as did audiences. Efforts to compete with television drove the movie industry to various innovations including Cinerama, Cinemascope, 3-D, and other venues. By the 1960s, the Hays Code had been replaced by a ratings system. The motion picture industry, now recognizing a newly emerging consumer audience, began creating films targeting that audience: adolescents. As motion pictures became increasingly hardcore adolescent, adults grew increasingly less interested in them.

Motion Pictures and Audiences Today

Other conventions also have changed. The regal old movie palaces have been torn down or turned into multiplexes, where refreshments account for a larger share of the profits than movie tickets and movies no longer change every week. Audiences have also become more fragmented, more homogeneous, often largely composed of young moviegoers between the ages of 12 and 29. According to the Motion Picture Association of America (MPAA; 1997), 12- to 17-year-olds, who today make up about 9% of the "resident civilian U.S. population, buy 14% of the movie tickets each week" (p. 1). In 1997, ticket buyers between ages 12 and 29 made up 49% of yearly admissions (MPAA, 1997). College-educated adults are more frequent moviegoers (30%) than those who graduated high school (23%) or those who did not complete high school (16%) (MPAA, 1997). However, fewer films are targeted at the tastes of more mature audiences. Today's weekly box office rounds out to 24 million tickets, in a population of over 220 million (MPAA, 1997).

Despite all that has changed, certain aspects of the movie experience have not changed. For most movie fans, going to the movies is an experience they still like to share with others—or with a significant other. In the dark, as they connect with the images and situations on the celluloid screen, they may still be conscious that there is a partner with them, they may still hold hands, they may still seek to share the magic. But they no longer take it for granted that the whole family can go out to see the same movie. In fact with the Hays Code gone, despite newer ratings systems, one cannot assume that most movies are safe for children. In any event, people no longer spend as much time at the movies, because the era of continuous showings of two films, a short, the news of the week, a cartoon, and the coming attractions is gone. People do not go out to the movies so much anymore; mostly, they go out to a movie.

Finding A Manageable Focus

Moviegoing as a Subculture

Modern, or postmodern, life offers American consumers a vast array of mediated in-home electronic entertainments from videos to computers, from television sports to satellite, from compact disks to digital video disks. It is not difficult in this world of easy technology to become a couch potato; the media marketing is awfully clever. But many movie fans preferred going out to see *Shakespeare in Love*, *Payback*, *Elizabeth*, or *Rushmore*, all 1998 movie hits, on a large screen in a commercial theater. They are not the vast majority of Americans, but their numbers and commitment to movies are certainly worth exploring. Members of this subculture take their moviegoing quite seriously. They are more likely to read reviews, and they are interested in movie talk. They follow news about films ranging from talk about the adaptation of a current novel, to whose performance or direction deserves an Oscar, to whether the Oscars mean anything, to gossip about actors, to advertising and marketing costs and strategies, to talk about genres. They like movie history; revisit old classics. They are often quite sophisticated about film production and conscious of the technical elements of film, such as camera work, editing, and sound.

Exploring Movie Encounters: The Necessity of an Interdisciplinary Approach

Moviegoing is a subjective experience, which, as an area of study, cuts across many related social science and communications disciplines: film audience research, motion picture history, marriage and family studies, leisure studies, interpersonal communication, ethnography and subcultural studies, motivational studies, and cultural studies.

In my original study (Matzkin, 1985), I had looked at the moviegoing conventions, attitudes, and experiences of a group of urban married couples over a 2-year period, to try to (a) understand their attitudes toward the medium, (b) explore their movie preferences, and (c) look at the nature of their joint movie encounters as they perceived them, as well as to explore whether urban moviegoers were different from rural or suburban ones. From the thousands of pages of taped interviews in which I had engaged, I analyzed their observations to determine the degree of activeness, using uses and gratifications theories suggested by Blumler and Katz (1974).

For this follow-up probe, I narrowed my focus to make it manageable. Although still focused on married movie fans, this time I was looking more narrowly at how they negotiate their movie dates. Still, questions that had cropped up in my previous research arose throughout the whole research process. What attracts us to certain films and film genres? Why do we avoid other kinds of films? How do couples balance each person's needs for certain kinds of leisure? Is moviegoing a ritualistic experience? What do these movie encounters mean in people's daily lives? Clearly, there were far more questions than time or space could begin to address in this study. There would have to be limitations.

Film Audience Research: An Underdeveloped Research Area

Although early motion pictures provoked excitement, they also provoked intense controversy over their possible negative effects on movie audiences, especially children. This resulted in a great deal of media research (see Charters, 1933). By the end of the 1940s, however, social science research had found more fertile ground for investigation in the newly emerging medium of television, and film audience research was eclipsed. Nearly 15 years after my own first disappointing investigation into this area of research, there is not much progress. My complaints follow those of Palmgreen and Lawrence (1991), which echoed Austin's (1983, 1989). Most film research today is conducted by the film industry for its own marketing and advertising purposes.

The Activeness Factor

One factor that seemed central in determining the meaning of the movie encounter in the world of married couples was the degree of activeness involved in the entire moviegoing process. Moviegoers can be perceived as active, because they are choosing to go out to a movie, as opposed to sitting at home and passively using a remote control clicker. They are also making other practical choices, including where (which theater) and when (time of day or night), arranging for child care, or even dog or cat care, and so on. Two other factors describing today's adult moviegoers seem to enhance the notion of a movie subculture. First, the literature tells us that moviegoers are clearly more selective about their movie choices in this generation than they were in previous generations. (Austin, 1989; Blumler & Katz, 1974). Second, today's grownups who go to the movies tend to be more educated than their nonmoviegoing age counterparts (MPAA,1997).

Examining the degree of activeness of moviegoers participating in this study seemed a manageable goal. I chose Levy and Windahl's (1985) activeness model as a beginning tool.

> Building on early work ... we will now develop a typology of audience activity. The typology is constructed from two orthogonal dimensions. The first—the qualitative orientation of audience members toward the communication process—has been given three nominal values: (1) selectivity, (2) involvement, and (3) utility. By "selectivity" we mean a process involving the nonrandom selection of one or more behavioral, perceptual, or cognitive media-related alternatives. We understand audience involvement to be first, the degree to which an audience member perceives a connection between him- or herself and mass media content; and, second, the degree to which the individual interacts psychologically with a medium or its messages. (p. 113)

Analysis would involve looking at how couples decide and select what they want to see (preexposure), how they encountered the movie experience (during exposure), and what their reactions were after viewing the film (postexposure). For this study, the greatest emphasis would be placed on how actively the interviewees pursue their movie encounters (negotiated the preexposure phase), although there would be some discussion of *during exposure* and *postexposure* issues as well.

The Problems of Quantitative Research

Getting at why people go to the movies, who makes the decision, and what significance, if any, it has in a couple's relating, involves questions that cannot easily be teased out through statistically formatted surveys or most forms of quantitative research. McQuail (1985) suggested that it was difficult to mechanize personal responses to media experiences. Blowers (1991) objected to ratings scales and other statistical methodologies because "the answers people give in questionnaires do not necessarily reflect what they feel, think or do in a situation which any particular question addresses" (p. 58). He also believed that media research should take into account the more complex and ambiguous reactions respondents have to experiences (p. 59).

Like Blowers and McQuail, Lindlof and Grodin (1990), although referring specifically to television audiences, expressed reservations about the value of ratings scales, which they perceived as ignoring the notion of "the multiple realities" involved in people's "every day engagements with television" (p. 10).

On the other hand, Lindlof and Grodin (1990) acknowledged a problem of using interviews because "in fundamental ways the conventions [of interviewing can] affect the quality and utility of its outcomes. To what extent might people not even be in touch with, or be unable to articulate, their basic feelings or beliefs about either the material they are viewing or about why they choose to do what they do?" (pp. 10–11).

Using observational studies also has drawbacks. Videotaping sufficient numbers of couples before they go out to the movies, during their moviegoing activity, and then afterwards is expensive, time-consuming, and awkward, although the results might be gratifying.

The Advantages of Qualitative Research

In support of qualitative research, Cantor (1987) concluded that "almost all social scientists have used interviews as either a primary or secondary means of collecting data. It can provide data often not available with other means. . . . In other words, interviews can provide knowledge about how people perceive their own conditions" (p. 256). Cantor warned here that perceptions can be manipulated by interviewers, interviewees, or the dynamics that evolve during the course of the talks.

Early mass media and communications studies in the 1940s, such as Berelson's (1949) study of the meaning of the newspaper in the life of readers and Herzog's (1944) research on daytime radio soap opera fans, were fascinating and humanizing glimpses into people's experiences, lives, and feelings. Such readable media studies, which often used personal interviews, dimensionalized the research and are looked at today as precious documents that transcend the specifics of the studies. I decided that my current research would again involve face-to-face interviews. I saw that this research could only begin to raise questions about complicated relational processes. Hopefully, others might be encouraged to pursue this line of inquiry.

Limitations of This Study

The limitations of such a research study are many: (a) This study does not address moviegoing in terms of media-effects theories or how movies influence attitudes, values, and beliefs. Instead, it looks at the ways in which people use movies. (b) Because this study is largely about self-reported responses, it cannot account for latent, out-of-awareness motivations that may be quite different from the explanations respondents provided. Subjectivity is a complex human phenomenon. (c) Regional differences may also exist, for example, one reason for going out to movies in commercial theaters might be that cable television is not an option. Approximately 30% of the U.S. population still does not have access to cable. (d) The population queried here was entirely White and middle-class. Further studies should include a more varied ethnic and racial cross-section of the married movie subculture. (e) Aside from its limited demographic scope, the size of the study sample is obviously rather small. On the other hand, adult moviegoers probably fit comfortably into this range of moviegoers, according to other surveys. This research is meant to encourage more discussion.

The Interviews

Description of Participants

A total of 24 married couples, who considered themselves movie fans, were interviewed in a variety of circumstances over a period of 3 months. However, 1 year later, at the 1999 Philadelphia Film Festival (while this research was being completed), I was able to interview 4 more couples briefly, which brought the number up to 28 pairs, or 56 individuals. All of the adult married couples were between the ages of 30 and 60 and lived in the Northeast, specifically in the New Jersey–Pennsylvania region. All were college educated, and some had advanced degrees. All were White and appeared to live in circumstances that would be considered middle- to upper-class. This raises the question of whether, in fact, adult moviegoing is becoming an elitist form of popular culture. Indeed, one study (Palmgreen & Lawrence, 1991) raised the issue of why there has not been more study of those who avoid going out to the movies.

All of the men in this study were executives, or in positions of authority or leadership in their professions. The women were highly educated and were or had been in the work world. Twenty of the couples had raised children, most of whom were now living out of the home. Only four couples of those queried had children under the age of 18.

The interviews ranged in length from approximately 20 minutes each, in the case of 12 couples interviewed at a hotel during a March 1998 Philadelphia Weekend Film Festival (and 4 couples at the same festival in February of 1999), to 1 hour each, in the case of 6 married couples in 1998, whose interviews were separately and privately audiotaped. A third group of 12 people (6 couples) were queried in rather brief 10- to 15-minute interviews during the course of a community event.

The audiotaped interviews provided more detailed contextual information regarding the ways in which couples negotiate their movie encounters. Male spouses in this group included a doctor, a social worker, a lawyer, two advertising/marketing executives, and a businessman. Several of the women were working artists, one was a real estate broker, one was an art-related businesswoman, and the other was a community leader.

The Interviewing Procedures

Because I wished to encourage my respondents to be candid, I asked them to participate in the interviewing process in an interactive style. The questions were organized to move from the more general and less complicated to the more personal and more provocative.

The interviewing began with a brief explanation of the purpose of the study. The first questions inquired about each couple's most recent moviegoing experiences: What had they seen, and when had they seen it? Aside from questions about the nature of their moviegoing encounters, couples were queried about their other uses of leisure time, their reading preferences, and their political proclivities.

Some General Findings

Two Clearly Different Groups Emerge

Despite the fact that almost all of the respondents perceived themselves as genuine movie buffs, or movie lovers, two somewhat distinct sets of moviegoing pairs emerged from this research. One smaller numbered group of couples, whom I have called *film buffs*, expressed a higher degree of activeness and intentionality in all aspects of their film experiences. A second, larger group of couples, whom I describe as *moderate moviegoers*, seemed more narrow in their film choices and expressed lesser degrees of commitment to the medium and to each of the phases of the moviegoing encounters.

Even within both of the groups, there was variation. Some film audience pairs seemed to be more actively involved in one phase than other phases; for example, some participated actively in the selection process and were less actively involved while watching the movies. Some did not like to reflect on them too deeply or seemed unable to recall much about films they had recently seen. Some would revisit a movie; others would not.

Movies Serve Many Purposes in Couples' Lives

Respondents interviewed for this study expressed an enormous appreciation for the medium and found many reasons for its attraction—from love for storytelling and narrative, to respect for its aesthetic elements, to a sense of enchantment with entering other people's lives in the darkened world of a theatre, to a simple desire for escape from the routine of their own lived worlds. Some sought a private interlude alone with their mates. Some felt there were "must see" movies that were getting a great deal of hype. Sometimes their moviegoing outings seemed to contradict reasons they gave for loving the film medium. For example, a couple who generally seemed selective in all phases of the encounter and who might normally rush to a foreign film like *Burnt by the Sun, Life Is Beautiful, Shakespeare in Love,* or the like might also choose to see a "no brainer" because it made few intellectual or emotional demands on them that particular day.

Despite both subtle and major differences in attitudes toward movies that distinguished film buffs and moderate moviegoers, there were, amongst this group of 56 people, many conventions shared by nearly all:

1. Overall, the respondents reported a strong preference for going to the movies with their marriage partner or some other companions as opposed to going alone. In most cases, neither partner normally attended movies alone.

2. More male than female spouses said they would not go out to a movie alone or without their partners, preferring to wait for films they might miss to be shown on TV. Wives, on the other hand, were willing to go out with friends because they preferred to see the movies in a commercial run. In a footnote to this, most of the pairs felt a need to save certain special movies to see with their mates and would have felt disloyal if they went to see such highly regarded movies without them.

3. Most film couples had a specific "agenda" when they went out to the movies. The agenda might be to see a light film, to unwind, or to see the latest seasonal hit.

4. Virtually all participants said they were motivated to see certain highly advertised mainstream movie hits. For example, half the respondents reported having seen the film *Titanic* before the 1998 Academy Awards had been announced and before it had been nominated as Best Picture.

5. Going out to the movies seemed to be an established ritual for each couple, which included different components for different couples. Some preferred going to movies and then out to dinner. Some preferred dinner followed by a movie. Some liked Sunday afternoon movies. One couple only liked going just the two of them.

6. One reason why most of the couples sought out certain movies and, often, mainstream hits was because they

felt a certain social pressure to be culturally current with the movie scene. Virtually all observed that the subject of movies came up frequently at a wide range of situations from work to cocktail parties and book clubs.

7. Most of the couples, but especially male respondents over 40, said they preferred going out to see a movie in theatrical release rather than renting videos. This preference might be related to the fact that from childhood, they had grown up with moviegoing as an established weekly ritual.

Preexposure: Negotiating the Movie Date

How movie couples choose their movie dates depends in part on their attitudes toward leisure time. Going out to a movie is not perceived by this subculture as a way of "killing time"; these couples are too busy and active for that, and leisure time is not taken lightly. Certain criteria will draw them most quickly to a film: the starring performers, directors, or genres; the adaptation of a novel they liked; even the way a film is marketed. Some of the couples found deciding what movie to see a joint ritual that was engaged in with thoughtful attention and eagerness, but which rarely created conflict. Others found choosing the right movie required more negotiation. Goals for their movie encounters differed not only from couple to couple but also in many cases from person to person. Overall, movie buffs tended to be more interested in seeing films by certain directors, whereas moderate moviegoers in general sought out movies starring favorite performers.

Movie Reviews

Movie pairs interviewed for this research expressed a wide range of opinions on how they use movie reviews. Movie buffs turned out to be more consistent readers of print news, both newspapers and magazines. About half of those interviewed read reviews (from newspapers, including the *New York Times, Philadelphia Inquirer*, and *Wall Street Journal*, and from magazines, including the *New Yorker*, *Time*, and *Newsweek*) and kept them in mind when choosing a movie outing. Some couples (fewer) were skeptical of reviews or said they did not like to have a review spoil the surprise of the story line or preferred reading them after seeing a film. For some couples, movie reviews were important even in cases where they did not have an especially high regard for the reviewers. This was explained because such moviegoers were able to glean decisive generic information about genre, script, themes, and mood from reviews.

The more committed to movies, the more the participants read reviews, which does not mean they were always influenced by what they read. In addition, more wives than husbands read reviews thoroughly, although in at least one instance, a female movie buff was adamant about not reading reviews fully until after seeing a film. Because some women were more informed, they often tended to have more input into the selection process of the movie date.

Movie Buffs Have an Easier Time Deciding on Which Movie

What couples decide to see on any given night does not necessarily represent their overall movie inclinations and tastes. Because of their appreciation for the film medium, movie buffs expressed enthusiasm about a wide range of films from slapstick to serious art films, from dramas to science fiction, from foreign films to mainstream adolescent "summer sillies." However, moderate moviegoers, because of their more limited, more circumscribed range of movie preferences, had to work out compromise movie arrangements more frequently. For example, there were more genres of films, such as slapstick, science fiction, action adventure, serious drama, or romantic "women" issues films, that one partner, usually male, wished to avoid. Certain themes or motifs, such as homosexuality or transvestism, also were perceived negatively. Finding a compromise film could take some complicated negotiation for such couples. Because movie buffs seemed to have a wider set of movie options, they found selecting a movie less conflicting. More buffs seemed to have compatible movie tastes.

During and After the Movie

Although these moviegoers had many years of married life together, those who participated in taped interviews were able to describe moments of annoyance with each other's movie reactions. Because they are aware of their partner's presence during movie engagements, they can usually pick up on whether their experiences are "in synch." Several wives mentioned that recognizing disparate reactions by their husbands while watching a movie could affect their own enjoyment, even if their husbands' reactions were pre-dictable. "Of course it affects me," noted one wife. "I always feel guilty if he doesn't like a film that I like, especially if I chose it."

One result of being "turned off" while watching a movie can be a lack of clear recall of many of the movie's scenes, images, or other details. Strongly differing interpretations or reactions could lead to disagreement and temporary distanc-ing between pairs. For some couples who experienced very divergent responses to a film, discussion (postexposure) might be brief, postponed, or avoided entirely. However, for the most discriminating of the viewers queried, disliking a film could also be an excellent opportunity for lively discus-sion, if the pair felt comfortable airing and sharing their dif-fering perspectives.

As noted previously, movies elicit strong reactions in view-ers. What is perhaps most complicated here and somewhat ironic about movie viewers' personal reactions is the strong sense of legitimacy they give to their perceptions, in contrast to their overall perceptions about other forms of art and en-tertainment. Because popular movie reviewers and movie criticism in general get a great deal of media publicity, people are familiar with movie reviewers often by name. In contrast, there is far less public and media attention paid to the re-viewing of literary works, theater, dance, rock concerts, or museum and gallery shows. Still, audiences who attend such events seem more willing to acknowledge that critics for dance, theater, literature, art, and painting may have illuminating observations to contribute on these art endeavors that may transcend their own. When it comes to movies, everybody believes he or she is a true and final critic. This sense of owning an interpretation can impact on movie pairs' disagreements, because such challenges to each other's perceptions can provoke self-esteem issues or a desire or need for validation.

Gender Differences

From the earliest aspects of negotiating movie dates to the last words uttered regarding the movie, there appeared to be noticeable gender differences, although among the couples perceived as movie buffs, the differences between husbands' and wives' movie inclinations were less distinct.

Male Preferences for Action–Adventure

With very few exceptions, male spouses indicated an interest, if not a preference, for seeing action–adventure films. These men tried hard to distinguish between adventure genre films they liked and those they perceived to be geared for children and adolescent males. Movies that were perceived as cartoonlike were less appealing than films by Clint Eastwood, Quentin Tarantino, or David Lynch, directors whose skills in cinematography, editing, and writing are highly regarded, despite the violence and shock value for which their screenplays also are well known. All male spouses reported they would happily see any film starring Harrison Ford or Harvey Keitel, two well-known actors associated with action–adventure movie genres.

However, the majority admitted that dramas and comedies have appealing qualities that stay with them longer than the typical action movie they say they prefer. Men explained the preference for action–adventure as a way of relaxing, unwinding, and escaping from occupational stress.

Female Flexibility

Nearly all the women expressed a dislike for science fiction, horror, or what they called "teenage violence" movies. Despite this disapproval of violence, women were more flexible in their movie selections, more willing to accommodate the movie choices of their spouses, even to see a film that was not their first choice, if it meant going out. Although the group of wives interviewed for this research had independent careers, they still expressed a preference for going out to the movies, as opposed to staying home and watching television or videos. Wives more willingly went to see films starring either favorite male or female actors. In contrast, husbands' choices were frequently dominated by their interest in seeing films with favorite male stars and were far less predisposed to movies that starred their wife's favorite female performers.

Fischoff, Antonio, and Lewis (1997) speculated on this phenomenon:

> It is not immediately clear why women show less of a dismissive attitude toward Action–Adventure movies than men show toward Romance movies. . . . Women were equally likely to favor a movie because of the lead actor or actress. . . . Men, on the other hand, showed a distinct gender preference and were significantly more likely to favor a movie because of a male lead than they were to favor a movie because of a female lead. . . . But clearly, when women's films comprise 38% of women's Top 25 list, while men placed no such films in their list, there is a substantial gender disparity. (p. 16)

This study suggests that in fact, "men and women . . . head to the theater together, but they want and need . . . different things from movies" (Palazzi, 1998, p. 61). Movie producers, and their advertising and marketing executives, pay close attention to these differences.

Gender-based theories are not new, of course, but is it an accurate assumption that action–adventure films with their high quotas of media violence are serving the biological male need for competition and dominance? Explanations suggesting that men prefer spatial images and women verbal images and that preferences for fast editing, objects moving in space, fast action, crashes, and noise have some sort of physiological and biological basis do appear to get a good deal of pop psychology attention. Palazzi (1998) quoted author Michael Gurian's interpretation of gender differences: "Males are set up in our society to prove themselves. . . . And there's another purely hormonal plus. . . . After seeing a violent film, a man experiences a surge of testosterone that's very pleasant for him" (p. 61). Fischoff et al. (1997) also concluded in their studies that as males age, their preferences for action–adventure decrease and their willingness to engage with more romance seems to increase (pp. 15–16).

The fact that virtually all of the men in this small study did occasionally agree to see movies their wives chose indicates that people can become more compromising. Moreover, wives interviewed here, while consistently more accommodating, said they felt able to assert their needs and inclinations.

Examples

The interviews were packed with interesting exchanges, which time and the limitations of this study can only suggest. However, I have provided a sampling of remarks from the audiotaped sessions, to demonstrate some of the types of issues that emerged.

Husbands Who Perceive Themselves as More Selective

Several of the male respondents who described their wives as having very "tolerant" or "flexible" attitudes and tastes in movies also perceived those wives as "less selective and less critical." These husbands described themselves as the more discriminating film viewers in the twosome. Male spouses with these views also had the strongest attraction and preferences for action–adventure films. (Illustrations are provided below as Couples 1 and 2.)

Couple 1. Couple 1 expressed wide-ranging differences in the kinds of movies that interested each of them. This husband, a high-powered business consultant, was very outspoken about his likes and dislikes.

> **Wife**: My husband likes action movies, and he doesn't care about who is producing them. He doesn't go to have a deep, stimulating evening. He goes to the movies to relax.
>
> **Husband**: I am going to satisfy you, baby.
>
> **Wife**: It's action, cops, and robbers, James Bond, or a very good mystery. Other stuff, more sensitive or in a foreign language, or too slow developing narratives are not as exciting . . . as with things happening every second. He's too tired and overworked, and he falls asleep. It is not a good time for him to get involved in a slow, beautiful movie.
>
> **Interviewer**: Do you go with different expectations or respond differently when you go to see live theater?
>
> **Husband**: Not if it is boring and slow. I usually fall asleep, or we leave at intermission.
>
> **Interviewer**: How do you define *boring*? Is it the subject matter, is it a script that is not well made? Is it if the script is slow in unveiling itself?
>
> **Husband**: My view of that is that it is their responsibility as the ones who wrote and produced and designed to make it intoxicating [for movies and for live theater]. I don't want to struggle to try to stay interested. If they cannot do it, tough! . . . My wife likes everything. She likes romances and artsy movies that are very slow and drawn out, and she likes movies about deep subjects that seem to ramble. She gets something out of these films, that I find hard to understand. My wife finds things she thinks are wonderful. Me, I need the whole gestalt.

Couple 2. As with Couple 1, Couple 2 negotiated their moviegoing on the basis of what the male partner would agree to, if he could not convince his wife to see an action–adventure. Going to a movie led to further moviegoing, in part because seeing the trailers could spark further interest.

Wife: Going out to the movies comes in a seasonal way whenever the new cluster of movies come out. We kind of mention them and say, "Hey, I heard that this was good" and make a list of what seems appealing. And he will usually say, "I DON'T WANT TO SEE THAT!" I always want to see the more artsy films, and he always wants to see the more action-oriented films.

Husband: Well, there are really three lists: what she will see, what I will see, and what we both will see. Generally what we both will see will win out. . . .

Interviewer: Are there some genres that either of you don't like to see?

Husband: I won't go to any romantic love stories. I've no interest in sitting through them.

Interviewer: Do either of you go alone?

Husband: Movies that I would go to but she won't, and I won't force her—ultimately they will come out on television—and then I will watch them.

Wife: I will go with a friend on a Monday night.

Interviewer: So neither of you go alone?

Husband: No . . . I can't sit still in a movie by myself for 2 hours. I may watch a movie on an airplane, because it kills time, but I would never, and I can't think of a situation in the last 50 years when I went by myself.

Interviewer: What do you go for most—story line, genre, director, actors?

Wife: I think we go for story line and actors.

Husband: It depends a lot on the review . . . I think.

Interviewer: So you read the reviews. Would you read a review of a movie you didn't want to see—such as the film version of [Henry James's] *Wings of the Dove*?

Husband: No, well, I wouldn't read a deep review.

Interviewer: Do you go to see foreign films?

Husband: No, not as a thing to do. If it is a film of interest, but not just because it's foreign.

Wife: Didn't you go to see *Il Postino* [an Italian film] with me?

Husband: Yes.

Interviewer: How was that for you?

Husband: I liked that movie.

Wife: There is another factor here. He is away all week and not interested in driving distances, or into the city after a long commute from out of town. So much wear and tear on the individual. In my case, there are certain stars that I am interested in seeing.

Husband: For me, a lot has to do with the promotion. Obviously advertising creates an interest or noninterest.

Interviewer: Have you ever been to a movie where you did not have the same reaction?

Wife: Always! Frequently! . . . It ruins it for me. He will stand up at the end and say, "That was the stupidest movie I ever saw," and I will still be totally engaged in the experience.

Husband: I'm entitled to my opinion.

Wife: You could wait an hour.

Husband: You asked me. . . . I find that the general rule is that my wife likes everything.

Wife: Not everything but more things than you.

Husband: And that I generally tend not to like most things because I have a lower tolerance, or a higher standard, or I am just not as much involved.

Compatibility Leads to Flexibility

The women queried in large part did not find slapstick comedy very funny. They went out to one of those "highly cha-

otic films" (as one woman described the genre) to accommodate their husband.

Couple 3. Partners were both flexible here.

> **Wife**: I really think there is a male–female thing about
> slapstick. He loves it. The reason I don't like slapstick is
> because when I see mayhem—I think about cleaning up.
> I think women need order in their world to survive and
> take care of their children.

Although Wife 3 did not enjoy most slapstick comedies, on
the whole, this couple seemed to have a very broad range of
film genres that they both enjoyed and, in any case, usually
joined the other without regret even at a film not his or her
first choice. Instead of going with an attitude of "I don't want
to be here," the outlook was, "I'm going to find something
good about this."

> **Husband**: I would say that going to the movies is some-
> thing that I have a very simplistic attitude about. De-
> pending on how I feel is whether I want to see something
> deep and involving and perhaps revelatory about the hu-
> man condition—a film like *Wings of the Dove*—or I might
> be at the other end—I just want to go out and have a
> good time. And in that case, I want to see one of two
> types of films: an action adventure as banal as James
> Bond or *Day of the Jackal* or a slapstick comedy like *The
> Naked Gun*. So, if I'm in the mood of "It's been a long
> week!" it's cop-out. Otherwise, I will go to something at
> the Ritz [the local Philadelphia art film theater].

> **Wife**: I would say you pull me in the direction of the
> action film a little more than I would probably go myself.
> But I enjoy a good action film. One thing we both agree
> on is that when films become total mayhem—they have
> to blow up everything and people are shot and there are
> no consequences—we both agree not to go.

> **Husband**: There were times when I had doubts about
> some small movies before going and found myself really
> getting involved with the character and found it so

worthwhile. Even though if given a free choice, I might have opted to go to see a film more in the action–adventure genre. For example, *Brassed Off*, *Shall We Dance?* and *Kolya* were terrific films. They were Ritz-type movies that were so endearing, and you really felt like you had sat through something worthwhile that you could remember and talk about and think about.

Wife: We try to save special movies, if he is out of town, for when we are together. I really think that films play a very important role in our lives. We see lots and lots of films, and we like very much to talk about them and the conflicts and interpretations, and we don't always agree, but that's half the fun of it.

Husband: It is definitely the literature of our time. . . . When we disagree, our differences of opinion are just a matter of degree. I thought that was wonderful—not so wonderful. We saw eight films over Christmas in Florida, and I think we agreed on all eight.

Wife: How telling is it that we were away for eight days and saw eight movies.

Couple 4. Couple 4 also are very compatible in their moviegoing inclinations. Like Couple 3, they try to see certain films together. They also take turns choosing films.

Wife: We go once a week, but sometimes we miss a week and go twice the next week, so it averages out to about once a week.

Husband: We usually like to go in the middle of the week—it breaks up the week for us.

Interviewer: Do you usually want to see the same movies?

Both: Yes, pretty much.

Wife: It's a joke in our house—someone picks, and the other says, "Okay I'll go, 'cause I'll probably want to see it." And if it's bad, the other gets the next turn. . . . In fact, I was just thinking that I will be away when he is away—he is going on business, and I am going to visit one of the children, and maybe we could both go to the movies while we are away and see the same film that we don't want to miss. It may be gone by the time we both get back to Philadelphia.

Husband: I am emotionally incapable of going to see a movie by myself. I think it is the loneliest thing in the world. You go into a dark film by yourself, and you don't have anyone to discuss it with. I think I may have done this once in the last 35 years. When she went on a trip with our daughter to India, and I decided that I would mentally play, "What would I do if I was single? How would I entertain myself, aside from a physical relationship, a Clinton experience?" I got myself a ticket to a Broadway play, and it was a marvelous play. But I thought it was the emptiest experience in the world because I didn't have anyone to talk to about it. Damn, this is just like going to the movies by yourself. The interplay back and forth of what did we really see? What were they trying to say? And our discussion back and forth.

Wife: The difference is I would easily go to a movie by myself, and while I would miss discussing it with him, I might call you up and discuss it or with another friend.

The Marketing of Movies

The significance of gender differences has not been lost on movie producers and their marketing designers. Increasingly, and with greater sophistication, they are utilizing different gender-directed strategies to sell the same movie. Miramax, L.A., for example, used gender-specific trailers in their movie ad campaigns for the 1996 Oscar award winning film, *The English Patient*, for which,

> the main campaign was aimed at women. It played up the film's epic love story and was set to beautiful music. The second ad, edited for a male audience, emphasized the wartime setting, the espionage, and the mystique of the Ralph Fiennes character. . . . Then Miramax turned to TV's Nielsen ratings. They aired the "female" ad during

> shows that are popular with women, and the "male" ad during shows with a large male audience. The system worked. *The English Patient* earned $78 million in the United States and $149 million overseas. (Palazzi, 1998, p. 63)

The emphasis on gender research is not reserved for motion picture advertising and marketing, but is an important component of television programming as well. Such research raises questions about the notion of shared media experiences.

> The consistency of that dynamic underscores how men and women watch television differently, as well as changes in a wired-for-cable world that contribute to such a rift, prompting many couples to adjourn to separate rooms and watch TV on their own. . . . Men are masters of the remote control, and they will surf more easily than women do. . . . Women were more than twice as likely to mention dramas among their favorite forms of programming, while four times as many men chose sports. Based on a breakdown of prime time network series, the current television season's No. 1 show among men, *Monday Night Football*, doesn't crack the Top 20 with women. (Lowry, 1998, p. D7)

Idiosyncratic Conventions Suggest Moviegoing Has Ritualistic Components

Couple 5. Although most filmgoers queried here observe the practical considerations of time, location, and convenience, as well as meal requirements, when planning their film encounters, certain couples have established habits that differ from others, even within their own social circles.

> **Husband**: Now that I think about it, going to the movies is definitely a part of the relationship. And you want it to be a good experience, and therefore you try to get together on the movie you both like.

> **Wife**: We have some friends that we have known for 25

years, and recently, we went to the movies all together. I found it so awkward, and I realized that I would rather go to the movies with just one other person, not with a whole crew. It was such a big deal getting everybody together. I was distracted.

Husband: I am not distracted like that. She is very easily distracted. The conditions have to be just right for Nancy to enjoy it.

Wife: There were too many people to please about where to sit, how close, what time, dinner, and on and on.

Husband: The women usually make the arrangements, so it becomes a complicated set of conditions that all have to operate together for it to be smooth.

Interviewer: How about with one couple?

Wife: We don't even do that. We get together with couples often because we like to go out. But movies are better—more intimate—with just the two of us.

Husband: Yes, we agree on that. We do see these other people. And when we get together, we do talk to them about the movies that we've seen. That's how we handle it.

Self-Reporting Does Not Always Reflect Self-Knowledge

Couple 6. One couple who had been audiotaped appeared to have contradictory views about how their movie dates are initiated.

Husband: I am probably the one who generally—60% of the time—initiates going to the movies.

Wife: That's not true. I will say to you, " Let's go to the movies." I would say that I initiate.

Interviewer: So you have a difference of opinion about who initiates.

Wife: When we do go to a film we become passionate,

and afterwards it becomes a heated discussion. Always. Nothing goes by us.

Husband: We don't want to see an average film.

Interviewer: How do you feel about foreign films?

Husband: We like them.

Interviewer: What if you wanted to see different movies?

Husband: We'd compromise. I'd see the one she wants.

Wife: Ha! Ha! It doesn't always work. Frankly, if I could go to my movie—and he could go to his at the same time in the same movie house—the concept doesn't make me uncomfortable.

Husband: We compromise before we get there.

Wife: I think I compromise more than you do, wouldn't you agree?

Interviewer: Do you think one of you has stronger feelings about moviegoing?

Husband: I read the reviews more regularly—I want to see the movies more.

Wife: He gets more committed. I have an optimism that anything is going to be somewhat exciting for one reason or another.

Husband: I know why I usually get to pick the movie. Because probably two thirds of the time she falls asleep during the movie.

Wife: Very funny.

Husband: Why don't we rent films?

Wife: I don't watch television.

Husband: Going out is nice. If I wasn't working full-time and I had more time, I would be renting more.

Discussion of Findings

More About the Two Types of Moviegoers Evolves

Movie buffs' greater sense of adventure and openness to various genres of films seemed to underscore differences in the ways they connect with many other kinds of experiences. Buffs were more likely to select a foreign film, a controversial film theme, a film dealing with complex social and political issues than were the more circumscribed moderate moviegoers. Buffs put more emphasis on seeing films whose directors they admire. Perhaps most distinctive about movie buffs is the way in which they engage with the films. Rarely passive spectators, their involvement during films is usually intense and leaves them eager for analytic after-movie talk. This was of interest to them, even when they felt the film they had seen was disappointing or unfavorable. They were therefore less likely to turn off during a film viewing and more likely to try to understand what about the film made it less than successful or made it not work for them.

One film buff husband (from Couple 3) expressed a series of contradictory notions about his moviegoing proclivities. This man is a voracious reader of sophisticated literary works as well as nonfiction. It was interesting that he described movies as "the literature of our time." He seemed to turn to reading for intellectual and aesthetic appreciation and to turn to action–adventure films when left to his own devices. However, because his wife clearly preferred more weighty films, he would accommodate her and then usually found the experience satisfying.

Moderate moviegoers (see Matzkin, 1985), as noted above, lesser risk takers, were more active in the preexposure phase of the process than "during exposure" aspects of the movie encounter. And, generally, one of the two partners was more committed to the encounter. Being more disposed to action–adventure genres, or big-budget, mainstream, highly marketed American films, they did not feel as much inclination to analyzing the films. Moderate husbands avoid "women's" movies (movies that focus on women's issues or are pointedly romance films) or movies dealing with controversial sexually oriented subjects, such as gay or lesbian sexual orientations. They were also resistant to viewing foreign films, which they complained are too slow moving. Moderate movie wives tend to be more flexible and less intense in their moviegoing proclivities and able to accommodate their husbands. They said they found opportunities to see those movies their husbands avoided with women friends.

Because for moderate moviegoers, going out to a movie could lead to temporary disengagement during the actual film encounter, when one of the two might express boredom or annoyance, or even fall asleep, their postexposure discussions were sometimes abbreviated, because of the divergencies in views or to avoid further conflict.

These findings mainly seemed to be consistent for the other two dozen briefer interviews, which included four younger couples (under 40) who had children living at home. Responses to questions regarding action–adventure films, movie reviews, foreign films, and issues of negotiation generally were parallel. However, there were some divergences.

The younger couples, particularly those who had children at home, tended to go out to fewer movies but rented more videos. Because they did not have the expectations of going out regularly (at least once a week) to see a movie, they indicated that they did not always pay as much attention to reviews but were aware of word-of-mouth, marketing, and the like.

Not all of the younger (40 or under) women had the same feelings about comedies or about action–adventures. At least two of the younger women interviewed (in the briefer queries) enjoyed them and sought them out, making their husband–wife moviegoing or video rentals quite compatible. In all groups, male spouses spent more time watching television than did wives.

Watching Videos

In fact, although all of the approximately three dozen people interviewed seemed to some degree actively engaged in going out to the movies, they were much less interested in renting movies at home. The hectic and demanding lifestyles of these discussants discouraged many from regularly using video rental outlets; tracking and returning films seemed too time-consuming. On the whole, the vast majority said they preferred going out and seeing movies on a big screen. There were some differences for men and women here.

Moviegoing and Politics

Finally, a strong correlation emerged between couples' moviegoing proclivities and their political views. This assessment evolved out of discussions both about movie interpretations and the several phases in the movie encounters. Movie buffs were clearly more predisposed to be identified as moderate or liberal Democrats. On the other hand, amongst moderate moviegoers, the more circumscribed their moviegoing proclivities, the more conservative their political views. In the cases of audiotaped couples, for example, Couples 1 and 2 were registered Republicans, with more conservative leanings. On the other hand, Couples 3, 4, 5, and 6 identified themselves as Democrats with moderate to liberal leanings. The male spouse of Couple 6 described himself as an independent but voted Democratic because of concerns about social issues. Among the other 12 couples interviewed, the breakdown was almost identical. Couples (generally movie buffs) who actively sought out innovative films, foreign films, serious films, and the like tended to be more politically liberal.

These findings support Adler's (1959) and Matzkin's (1985) studies of art film audiences and their intellectual and political leanings. Film buffs appear to have a higher interest in films that are stylistically innovative, which approach or contemplate subject matter, characters, and stories from unpredictable or more philosophical perspectives. This comfort with more complex subject matter attracts them to foreign films, which often use slower editing rhythms and greater subtleties, textures, and shadings. Movie buffs tend to reject notions of life in rigid terms of black or white. Their more probing predilections make them more comfortable with controversial, innovative, or experimental works in music, theater, or the visual arts as well. That these proclivities also correlate to political leanings seems both relevant and predictable.

Some Problems of the Findings

During the 1998 annual Philadelphia Weekend Film Festival, a 2- or 3-day affair held in early March that usually involves a film retrospective centered around one creative artist in the Hollywood film world, I spent several hours attempting (on different days and evenings), between film viewings, lectures, video clips, and formal discussions, to query this seemingly rich research population. The festival was, on this particular occasion, honoring actor–producer Richard Dreyfuss, who was present as a guest for the entire weekend at the hotel where the events were held. Screenings of his films were ongoing during the weekend, including one for *Mr. Holland's Opus* (1996).

That screening, held at 11:00 p.m., was attended by 17 out of the 200 persons attending the festival, most of whom described themselves as film enthusiasts. Because the festival members had paid extravagantly to attend the weekend, the issue of how open and candid at least some filmgoers are about their own movie interests may be problematic.

A postscript on this observation emerged after my attendance at the Philadelphia Weekend Film Festival of February 27 and 28, 1999. Here, the honoree was the highly acclaimed Meryl Streep, who has been nominated for Best Actress at the March 1999 Academy Awards ceremonies, for her performance in the screen adaptation of the Anna Quindlen novel, *One True Thing*. The Philadelphia weekend was a sellout way in advance, and demand for hotel rooms and entry was oversubscribed. The majority of those who came to pay tribute to Streep had neglected to see her other major film of the year, *Dancing at Lughnasa*. However, there was a far greater number of attendees who stayed up past 11:00 p.m.

to watch at least part of the midnight movie, *Postcards From the Edge,* which starred Streep along with Shirley MacLaine. About 35 attendees out of almost 250 weekend guests stayed up to watch the film, seeming to underscore the earlier observations that performers and celebrities are more compelling reasons for either watching movies or attending a movie festival than directors and that many people who consider themselves movie buffs more likely are star struck.

Moviegoing and Today's Youth

As we know, young people still go out to the movies, and MPAA (1997) figures tell us that the percentage of movie tickets sold each week continues to be far and away higher for young people between the ages of 12 and 25 than it is for all other age groups. Whether this trend will continue is not entirely clear.

> Underneath any immediate optimism about the potential box-office boost that *Jurassic Park* and *Last Action Hero* could lend to the summer is a real anxiety about the continuing decline in the movie going audience—specifically the all-important 13–25 year old segment. . . . The fact is that young people in 1983 accounted for 55% of all tickets sold—way above their proportion of the population. (Fox, 1993, p. F1).

The article went on to say that according to the Motion Picture Association of America, in 1992 young people only accounted for 38% of ticket sales.

Young people do perceive movies as a relational experience. According to the results of a small survey of college students taken in April 1998 at Abington College, Penn State University, more than 90% of those queried preferred going to the movies with someone, preferably a romantic partner.

To analyze the survey, I used a statistical program package intended primarily for social sciences, SPSS 8.0. I assigned each question a variable label and coded the answers to the questionnaire numerically for entry into a database. Although the sample size, 51, was relatively small, the results are indicative of general trends in moviegoing of younger audiences. However, further study is needed to lessen the variability in the results.

1. None of the students queried expressed a preference for going to movies alone. (Three persons in combination with other preferences said that they would go alone.) Ninety-six percent of the respondents always preferred to go to the movies with someone, and 58.9% included going to the movies with a romantic partner in their response.

2. 84% consider moviegoing a dating convention.

3. 68% said they were not worried about choosing a movie for themselves and their partner to see because the partner might not feel the same about the movie.

4. 58% said that there are certain types of movies that they avoid seeing.

5. 84% said movie dates were determined choices by compromise once in a while, which could result in seeing a film that she or he was not really interested in seeing, 12% said that they would always compromise, and 4% said that they would never compromise.

6. 76% said that they were aware of their companion's response.

7. 88% answered that their best movie companion has similar tastes in movies.

8. 43% said the cost of going out to the movies discourages them.

9. 54% had a strong disagreement about a movie with a favorite movie companion; 44% said they had not.

10. 69% go occasionally out to the movies; 31% go frequently.

11. 67% consider *occasional* moviegoing to be once or twice a month; 64% consider *frequent* once or twice a week.

12. 92% said that they try to see anticipated movies with special movie partners.

Implications for Future Research

This study probably raises more questions than it answers; many of these questions deserve fuller exploration by psychologists. Here are just a few: Why is it that some find their life companions the best movie mates and others do not? Can moviegoing be considered in any way a litmus test for marital compatibility? What can our personal moviegoing inclinations and proclivities reveal about us as individuals? What does it mean if one can appear to respond openly to emotional experiences reflected on the celluloid screen but not to a parallel real-life human experience? What contribution to our own cultural mythmaking does moviegoing provide to the world?

The Age of Cinema dawned at the very turning of the nineteenth into the twentieth century. As we speculate about the future of cinema at the dawn of the twenty-first century, it seems appropriate to speculate as well on the future course of popular culture, of entertainment technologies, and of the uses of leisure. Will people still go out to a movie seeking romance, adventure, escape? Or, will we instead be spending even more time at home in front of computers and video screens and less time connected to other people, communities, and the outside world? What new narrative forms and technologies will emerge that create stories and myths, weave spells, touch daily life, and transcend it? Will the future's popular arts help engage and connect us, or serve further to divide our drifting and seemingly disparate civilizations?

References

Adler, K. P. (1959, Summer). Art films and eggheads. In E. C. Ulliassi (Ed.), *Studies in public communication* (pp. 7–15). Chicago: University of Chicago Press.

Austin, B. (1983). *The film audience: An international bibliography of research.* Metuchen, NJ: Scarecrow Press.

Austin, B. A. (1989). *Immediate seating: A look at movie audiences.* Belmont, CA: Wadsworth Publishing.

Berelson, B. (1949). What missing the newspaper means. In P. F. Lazarsfeld & F. N. Stanton (Eds.), *Communication research* (pp. 111–128). New York: Duell, Sloan & Pearce.

Blowers, G. H. (1991). Psychological approaches to film audience research. In B. Austin (Ed.), *Current research in film audiences, economics and law* (Vol. 5, pp. 56–67). Norwood, NJ: Ablex.

Blumler, J., & Katz, E. (Eds.) (1974). *The uses of mass communications: Current perspectives on gratifications research.* Beverly Hills, CA: Sage.

Cantor, M. G. (1987). Commentary on qualitative research and mediated communications in subcultures and institutions. In T. Lindlof (Ed.), *Natural audiences: Qualitative research of media uses and effects* (pp. 253–261). Norwood, NJ: Ablex.

Charters, W. W. (Ed.) (1933). *Motion pictures and youth: The Payne fund studies.* New York: MacMillan.

Fischoff, S., Antonio, J., & Lewis, D. (1997, August). *Favorite films and film genres as a functions of race, age, and gender.* Paper presented at the 105th Annual Convention of the American Psychological Association, Chicago.

Forsdale, L. (1976). *Every film is a Rorschach test* (2nd ed.). New York: Columbia University, Teachers College.

Fox, D. (1993, June 8). Honey, they shrunk the movie audience: Coveted under-25 group may be using video rentals, video games, while aging baby boomers attend less. *Los Angeles Times,* p. F1.

Herzog, H. (1944). What do we really know about daytime serial listeners? In P. F. Lazarsfeld & F. N. Stanton (Eds.), *Radio research (1942–1943)* (pp. 3–43). New York: Duell, Sloan & Pearce.

Levy, M. R., & Windahl, S. (1985). The concept of audience activity. In K. E. Rosengren, L. A. Wenner, & P. Palmgreen (Eds.), *Media gratifications research* (pp. 109–122). Beverly Hills, CA: Sage.

Lindlof, T. R., & Grodin, D. (1990). When media use can't be observed: Some problems and tactics of collaborative audience research. *Journal of Communication, 40*(4), 8–28.

Lowry, B. (1998, April 14). "La difference" in TV viewing habits. *Philadelphia Inquirer,* p. D7.

Matzkin, R. G. (1985). *The film encounter in the life world of urban couples: A uses and gratifications study.* Unpublished doctoral dissertation, Columbia University, Teachers College, New York.

McQuail, D. (1985). With the benefit of hindsight: Reflections on uses and gratifications research. In M. Gurevitch & M. K. Levy (Eds.), *Mass communication yearbook* (pp. 125–141). Beverly Hills, CA: Sage.

Motion Picture Association of America. (1997, July). *Incidence of motion picture attendance among the adult and teenage public: Highlights of find-ings*. Princeton, NJ: Opinion Research Corporation International.

Palazzi, L. (1998, May). Mars and Venus at the movies. *New Woman*, 61–63.

Palmgreen, P., & Lawrence, P. A. (1991). Avoidances, gratifications, and consumption of theatrical films. In B. Austin (Ed.), *Current research in film audiences, economics and law* (Vol. 5, pp. 39–55). Norwood, NJ: Ablex.

Personals. (1998a, May). *Philadelphia Magazine*, pp. 171–174.

Personals. (1998b, May 8–14). *Philadelphia City Paper*, pp. 102–103.

Pitock, T. (1997, November 9). Movies are too often the end of a beautiful friendship. *The Philadephia Inquirer*, p. E7.

6

Family Myths and the TV Media: History, Impact, and New Directions

Patricia Pitta

Myths have been with us since the beginning of time, and all cultures and religious groups have a mythology. The writers of these stories have sought explanations for the unexplainable or have wished to impart messages to others. We still develop myths to help forget difficult times by creating for ourselves a more pleasing world. Myths express our fears, desires, and hopes and are often fantasy solutions to seemingly unresolvable problems. Television in the 1950s and 1960s followed this formula in its presentation of American life. The Great Depression and World War II left people with a feeling of hopelessness and a desire for an ideal world, so we developed the myth of "the American Dream," which we hold onto till today. Now, we are about to embark on a 40-year historical journey through television, its impact on viewers, how programming has changed with the times, and possible new directions. The programs I chose to discuss are the programs I watched through my childhood and my adult life.

History

The idealized decade of the 1950s was perhaps a response to the 1929 stock market crash, which brought economic constraints and emotional pain to those living in the 1930s. Painful separations from family members and food and housing shortages were their constant companions. Men left to fight in World War II while women struggled to support their families. After the war, women were expected to return to the kitchen and reinstate the husband as head of household. Women silently accepted their fate, but a struggle was taking root and would spring to life in the early 1960s. Adults of the postwar era needed a break from their struggles and suffering, but war would not leave the American consciousness; Korea soon followed. Perhaps suburban families were capitalism's answer to Communism's threats of nuclear war and the advances of Sputnik. People started to fear moon exploration and being overtaken by Communism. In those years, the fear of nuclear attack was so strong, Americans built bomb shelters in their basements while Nikita Khrushchev and Richard Nixon met in the "Kitchen Debates" to try and stave off nuclear warfare. We sought relief from reality through material goods and "plastic" values. America needed to hold on to an ideal that would provide new hope. The idealized views of life we created for ourselves were reflected in the television programs of the time, values that would provoke the youth rebellion of the 1960s and 1970s.

What was the source feeding the family myths of the 1950s and 1960s? For centuries, the Protestant ethic had promoted work and family togetherness and dictated morality with little regard for the emotional development of individuals and families (Whyte, 1956). Individuals had their prescribed roles: Women took care of the home and children while men went out to work. Children should be seen, not heard, and discipline was severe. People other than those belonging to the White Protestant group were underdogs, and opportunity was largely unavailable to them other than to serve the so-called privileged class. Unfortunately, people of color were given little opportunity; their only function was to serve others. For most of them, their living conditions were unsatisfactory, to say the least, and the observance of their human rights virtually nonexistent.

The ready availability of material goods in the 1950s and

the time and energy devoted to obtaining them contributed to families' rising expectations and changing views. The plastic society began building a thick veneer, which it presented as fulfillment of the American Dream, the dream that would shatter the basic structure of the American family and society as a whole.

Separation of extended families contributed to the new malaise. With business opportunities booming and freedom to travel, families moved to the suburbs or out of state. When extended families did get together, they had unrealistic expectations of the family harmony and joy previous generations had experienced when family members tended to live within a stone's throw of one another. Many of these meetings were fraught with unexpressed anger and aggression, which were covered by socially appropriate behavior. Television shows of the 1950s and early 1960s reflected this, rarely showing families fighting, angry, or overwhelmed with each other. Television shows acted as models for "the way it was supposed to be" (Barnow, 1975).

Impact

Divorce

There was no room for divorce in the 1950s and 1960s media, even though nearly a third of marriages contracted in the 1950s ended in divorce in the 1960s and 1970s. A million married couples were separated in the 1950s, and many men began fleeing their marriage when their children left the home (Coontz, 1992). Feminism was in part a response to this emotional and financial abandonment. By the 1970s, no-fault divorce had become legalized, putting more emphasis on marital happiness rather than looking for who was to blame for its failure. The emphasis on long-term marriages was changing, marriages were becoming shorter in duration, and people were looking for happiness. "Studies of marital satisfaction revealed that more couples reported their marriages to be happier in the late 1970s than did so in 1957, while couples in their second marriages believed them to be much happier than their first ones" (Coontz, 1992, p. 16). The media reflected these trends. In the 1950s, there was not a TV show that recognized divorce; it was felt to be a disgrace and a failure. Popular opinion held that children without two parents were lost and had many problems, but it rarely considered children coming from intact homes who had problems as troublesome as those of children of divorce.

Although such programs as *The Doris Day Show* and *The Andy Griffith Show* of the 1950s featured a widow and a widower, respectively, it was not until the 1970s that shows focused on divorced families. One such example is *One Day at a Time*, in which a thirty-something divorced woman moved to a city with her two teenage daughters. Although Ann Romano struggled with being a mother, worker, and sole parent, this show broke the ice by demonstrating an alternative family style as a viable option. The protagonist had to deal with starting a new life and developing her own career while rearing adolescent girls on her own. Ann's struggles had no relation to those of the traditional family. She worked as a secretary and then decided to go to college when one of her daughters was beginning college. After many trials and tribulations, Ann received her degree and started a career in advertising, eventually becoming a partner in the new agency. She began the series with little education and status and worked her way into the middle class (Lichter, Lichter, & Rothman, 1994, p. 127). However, as in life, her struggles and numerous roles made for a life of frantic activity and workaholism, which culminated in a heart attack. The show demonstrated real problems facing this new alternative family system.

Beginning in the 1980s, divorced families were widely represented in the television media. For instance, *Who's the Boss?* featured a single working mother trying to maintain harmony in her household while supervising a single-parent housekeeper and a meddling sex-starved mother. *The Golden Girls* featured three divorced women, all over 50, living together with the outspoken, widowed mother of one of them.

Not only divorce but also sexuality and romance in older adults had gained acceptance.

Bachelors and Bachelorettes

Bachelors in the 1950s were categorized as immature, infantile, narcissistic, deviant, or even pathological (Coontz, 1992). Not until the late 1970s did shows appear that featured bachelors. An example is *Three's Company*, in which a single man lived with two women and pretended he was gay, so the landlord would allow him to live in the apartment. Though unrealistic in many ways, this show was an icebreaker for the American viewing public. In the 1980s, *House Calls* featured a single man who had an eye for the ladies, including his administrative assistant. Romantic chemistry was an overriding theme in the show.

As the 1980s moved into the 1990s, bachelors were depicted in a more sensitive manner, defying traditional roles. In *Full House*, a widower was joined by a single male relative and friend to care for his children. This show demonstrated responsible, caring, and nurturing men in nontraditional parenting roles functioning in an integrated manner. In the 1990s, the highly successful and very funny *Seinfeld* revolved around a group of shallow, neurotic, single friends, three male and one female, whose humorous interactions deflected the pain of their situations as they attempted to problem solve. Shows featuring single men still constitute a small percentage of television offerings. However, bachelorhood is no longer seen as a diseased state, but rather a natural stage of life and development. Bachelorettes made their debut in the late 1960s and early 1970s on such shows as *Three's Company*, *Laverne and Shirley*, and *Charlie's Angels*. These shows depicted single women living on their own, who not only enjoyed their sexuality but had to support themselves, and did so, breaking the image of women as dependent creatures.

Gay Men and Lesbians

Up until the early 1980s homosexuality was a theme that was absent from network TV. The show *Love Sidney* starring Tony

Randall as a homosexual commercial artist who played surrogate father to an aspiring actress and her illegitimate daughter was the first network show to work with the theme of homosexuality. The show was seen as quite controversial. It was not until April 1997 when Ellen DeGeneres came out of the closet on the sitcom *Ellen* that the networks allowed the theme of homosexuality to air again. And again, there was much controversy. Her show, as well as her personal life, received a great deal of media coverage and stirred up national conversation on gay and lesbian issues. It appears that programmers are finally ready to take risks and present alternate lifestyles and sexual orientations in a way that is entertaining and, at the same time, promotes understanding. Gay and lesbian groups interviewed by the media expressed their satisfaction with finally being acknowledged and presented favorably by the media.

Family Makeup

The makeup of families portrayed on television changed as well over the decades. In the 1950s, middle-class men were encouraged to marry; the lack of a suitable wife could mean the loss of a job or promotion (Riley, 1987). Societal rules were strict; every middle-class couple was "required" to have 2.2 children and a house with a white picket fence. Some critics have claimed that *All in the Family* was the first show to bring reality to the small screen no matter how vulgar the image presented. Archie Bunker was "an equal opportunity bigot, a no holds barred conservative, a last gasp holdout of an endangered species. Twenty years earlier audiences would have nodded in sympathetic agreement with his beliefs, laughing with him rather than at him" (Sackett, 1993, p. 183). On this show, characters expressed their anger and frustrations within marriage and between the generations.

Shows of the 1980s and 1990s have followed suit, depicting life as it is: intact families attempting to resolve their problems. Examples include the *Cosby Show, Family Ties, Growing Pains, Roseanne, Beverly Hills 90210, Married With Children,* and *The Simpsons*. The *Cosby Show* presented a Black functional family who dealt with such realistic problems as discord between parents and children, and resolution was accomplished. *Growing Pains* offered a look at the life of a mental health professional (psychologist) who had struggles like everyone else in his relationships and with family. Worthy of note is that some resolutions were not the "ideal." Members of this television family were able to say and act as they felt even if their parents did not agree. The public responded favorably to *Roseanne's* irreverent treatment of family and relationships. The viewing public felt that this show depicted people's neurotic pulls and interactions in a realistic manner and represented much of what goes on behind closed doors. Roseanne let it all hang out, literally and figuratively!

The reaction of many to *Married With Children* was how disrespectful it was of marriage and family. The marital bond was derided and desecrated as an institution. The parent–child bond was hopelessly confused, and developmental progress (career and emotional) in the younger generation was not realized. The characters made fun of each other in sadistic ways and did nothing to meet each other's needs, leaving each family member in a needy condition with a negative perception of life and the world. This was the longest running sitcom in the history of television. Is this show illustrating the many who have not been able to express their feelings or are unaware of their frustrations with family life?

The Simpsons, a very long running animated sitcom, appeals to people of all ages. A real attempt is made to resolve everyday problems and improve the human condition. Viewers watch for many reasons, among them the animation and identification with the characters, particularly Homer, a downtrodden figure who struggles to stay motivated to enjoy his work and who keeps trying to do the right thing. Freud (1919/1959, p. 391) pointed out that the repetition compulsion is alive and well within all of us. Homer exemplifies that as he tries to keep getting it right.

Full House featured male single-parent families whose relatives and friends helped with the parenting of three female children, demonstrating that patriarchal caregiving could be sensitive, nurturing, effective, and efficient. *Beverly Hills 90210,* another very long running show, deals with relation-ships among teenagers and young adults with each other and their families. The young (age 11-20) are attracted to this show because it deals realistically with the struggles teen-agers have with their families and presents many of the unex-pressed feelings, problems, and emotions of everyday life. It appears that the most popular programs voice the things most of us are uncomfortable expressing, which are locked within our minds and hearts. Self-realization is necessary if we are to reach our fullest potential as human beings.

As one can see, alternative ways of living are becoming well accepted and even sought after. The TV media plays a significant role in persuading society to accept new ways of looking at life and relationships. These shows demonstrate how a family's makeup can be different and function well in nontraditional ways.

Gender Roles

Gender roles changed on television to reflect changes in so-ciety. In the late 1940s, the print media questioned women's restlessness and presented feminism as a deep illness. Arti-cles in 1954 issues of *Esquire* and *Life* magazines, as described in *The Way We Never Were* (Coontz, 1992, p. 32), proclaimed, "Working women are a menace," and a *Life* magazine author termed married women's employment a "disease." Women who continued to seek employment were accused of engag-ing in the symbolic castration of men. Some states gave hus-bands total control over family finances (Miller & Nowak, 1975). This continued the nineteenth-century legal view of women as property of their husband. Women who worked for scant wages during the Depression and in wartime were expected to give up their roles and forget how to be success-ful outside the home. It is interesting that after women were encouraged to help the family in the difficult 1930s and war-torn 1940s, amnesia was required to adapt to the new ide-alized image of society. The majority of women followed the new rules, and by the late 1950s, tranquilizer and alcohol use among women was on the rise as they attempted to quiet their resentment and discontent.

In the 1950s and 1960s, women's roles were rigidly defined: Women stayed home and took care of the children while their husbands earned the money. Women were emotional and weak, whereas men were strong and silent. Women sought family happiness; men sought success. Acceptance of domesticity was the mark of middle-class status and upward mobility its hallmark (Warren, 1987). Women who could not walk the fine line between nurturing motherhood and castrating "momism" or who had trouble adjusting to "creative homemaking" were labeled *neurotic, perverted,* or *schizophrenic* (Warren, 1987).

Betty Friedan's (1963) book, *The Feminine Mystique,* considered to be the hallmark of the women's movement, provided answers for many. It encouraged women to view their options in life from new and different perspectives. Women began to see that they had important roles outside the home while reworking their responsibilities within it. In the early days of television, women were generally shown as "ditsy" or frustrated housewives subjugated to men, as in *The Honeymooners, I Love Lucy,* and *The Danny Thomas Show.* In all of these shows, the male will was dominant, and the woman always tried to please. Danny Thomas's real wife left the show after 3 years because she did not want to play second fiddle to her husband or children. Although women were often the butt of jokes, they gave strength and direction to the family unit.

In the late 1960s and early 1970s, the roles of women on television began to be reworked, reflecting women's attempts to be recognized in roles other than that of the dutiful wife. For instance, on the show *Julia,* Diahan Carroll played a nurse. This was the first show to feature a Black, female professional as the main character. On *The Doris Day Show,* Day was a widow who went to the big city to work and bring up children. Previously, women who found themselves in this situation moved back with their parents to nurture the children and, ultimately, their aging parents. The *Mary Tyler*

Moore Show was considered the perfect series for the liberated woman of the 1970s. It celebrated single, working, independent womanhood. Up to this point, it was customary for women to stay in their parents' home until they married. Here was a strong new message that a woman could live on her own and be responsible for her own welfare. Mary Tyler Moore was a positive role model for nontraditional women.

On the show *Maude*, the main character was the absolute antithesis of the Archie Bunker character, the show from which it was a spinoff. Many of its plots focused on women's independence and the rights of the modern woman. According to Lichter et al. (1994), the focus of the show was not quitting, but preserving one's rights. *Laverne and Shirley* featured two young women who worked as bottle cappers and shared an apartment while husband hunting. Even single, blue-collar female workers could be independent and have the ability to choose their financial and emotional fates. The 1970s also brought us *Phyllis*, a widow who found a job as a photo assistant, remarried, and lived with her disapproving mother-in-law. This show gave a bird's-eye view of Phyllis's attempts to deal with an enmeshed intergenerational system of mother and son. As discussed earlier, in *One Day at a Time*, a single divorcee left for the city to work and bring up two teenagers. On *Alice*, a widow took her son and went West in search of a singing career and, instead, found herself. Alice became the outspoken champion of blue-collar working women, providing another role model for women seeking emotional, financial, and psychological meaning in their lives. On *Flo*, a waitress with three failed marriages successfully transformed a run-down restaurant into her dream café. These 1970s programs were saying that it was all right to have an imperfect family and that women could seek alternative family lifestyles that might offer fulfillment.

"Under pressure to tone down the violence of 1970s cop shows, the networks found an alternative audience grabber in a genre most succinctly described as 'T & A TV' " (Lichter et al., 1994, p. 118). *Charlie's Angels* was representative of this trend, which featured scantily dressed female detectives who overcame danger each week. This was clearly a role change for women, although critics claimed the show perpetuated the stereotype of women as sex objects. In any case, women were finally getting out of the kitchen!

In the 1980s, shows became more probing and rich as the lives of single women functioned in new ways. *Kate and Allie* focused on two divorced women with three children who moved into Greenwich Village. Kate went out to work while Allie stayed home and took care of the kids. This was a new twist on house management that actually worked. In one episode, Kate and Allie attempted to fight the system by getting involved in a student protest when they discovered that a local university had invested in a chemical company charged with violating environmental safety regulations. Unfortunately, Kate and Allie went to jail for their actions, demonstrating "one can't beat the system," but clearly, the message to women was fight for your beliefs! The 1990s brought us *Murphy Brown*, a journalist with a child and no husband who managed a full-time career as well, and *Designing Women*, who sometimes dealt successfully with everyday problems while at other times attempted to work out relationship problems within the set of a profitable interior design business. This season's (1998–1999) *Ally McBeal* is a single, female lawyer portrayed as neurotic, finding herself in life situations that become overwhelming, dramatic, and funny. The show attempts to show how Ally tries to deal with her psychological and real-life problems. Some problems are dealt with, but others remain unresolvable. These programs depict women as competent and capable of managing their careers, for the most part, but struggling financially and emotionally in relationships. A man is no longer an essential component of a woman's identity and necessary to her credibility. As the commercial says, "You've come a long way baby." Women have changed the tapestry they weave in their jobs, homes, and hearts.

The Romantic Myth: Soap Operas

Although the soap operas have typically included such timely issues as single motherhood, gay and lesbian sexual orientation, AIDS, and breast cancer, their principal theme as

I see it is romantic encounters. The soap opera, the daytime companion to millions of women, offers a romantic view of life in which the protagonists do not work but spend the majority of their time continuing the myths of childhood fairy tales: socializing women to the oedipal paradigm (Livingstone & Liebes, 1995). One can compare a fairy tale to a soap opera. The fairy tale focuses on adventure and action, whereas the soap opera emphasizes emotions and relationships. Fairy tales have endings, whereas soap operas are open-ended (Mumford, 1994). Livingstone and Liebes (1995) have reported that soap operas focus on having never-ending narratives. Missing a mother, dependence on men, self-destruction in women, failure of romantic and nurturing relationships, and impermanence of marriage are consistent repetitive themes. The soap operas offer no solutions to the problems that make for constant emotional turmoil and despair. Everyday-life management is taken care of, and romance and business take center stage. The processes of managing daily life are invisible. Children and babies are almost absent in the soap opera. To further the case of nonendings and fantasy, people who are thought to be dead are reincorporated, having suffered from amnesia (Groves, 1983).

It is felt that soap operas reinforce traditional and stereotypical women's roles and would have viewers believe that the world of the soap opera resembles the real world. Sexual encounters happen between the unmarried without negative consequences (Larson, 1996), and women constantly fight over the same man. Female identity and value are attained through relationships with men. When one does encounter a female professional, she is using her professional status to get the attention of a romantic interest. Soap operas' portrayal of romance present women in a very needy manner. But viewers continue to watch avidly, to leave their dull, predictable lives for some romance and glamour.

The Extended Family

The American Dream was being realized by many (Coontz, 1992). Even the images of Hollywood stars were reworked to show their commitment to marriage and stability, as seen in the movies of Doris Day, Gregory Peck, and Fred Astaire. TV colluded with the American Dream to present the well-to-do middle class rather than the real-life situations of the real middle class and the poor.

> Twenty five percent of Americans, forty to fifty million people, were poor in the mid-1950s. At the end of the 50s, a third of American children were poor. Sixty percent of Americans over 65 had incomes below $1,000 in 1958, considerably below the $3,000 to $10,000 level considered to represent middle-class status. In addition, a majority of the elderly lacked medical insurance. Only one half of the population had savings in 1959; one quarter of the population had no liquid assets at all. Even when we consider only native-born white families, one third could not get by on the income of the household head. (Coontz, 1992, pp. 29–30)

As we can see, there was a great deal of strife and poverty in the 1950s, which the media denied in its portrayal of the American family. Idealizing the nuclear family, shows of the 1950s and 1960s ignored the extended family. In the late 1950s and during the 1960s, in shows such as *The Real Mc-Coys, Andy Griffith, Petticoat Junction, Green Acres,* and *The Beverly Hillbillies,* grandparents were an integral part of the family. In other shows, as in society during the 1950s and 1960s, the extended family virtually disappeared except for perfunctory holiday get-togethers. The child and the nuclear family became the basic family structure. With this loss of support from the extended family, mental health professionals were needed to provide what the extended family had, before the rush of upward mobility and the mass exodus to the suburbs.

Children

Children played a special role in television's families of the 1950s and 1960s. They were given time to play, and gentle maternal guidance replaced the patriarchal authority of the past. The focus of the family became the child because parents wanted to give their children everything they were deprived of as a result of growing up post-Depression and postwar. After World War II, the economy was favorable and much was possible for the baby boomers, who were to experience life as it had never been experienced by their parents.

Programs like *Leave It to Beaver* and *Father Knows Best* focused on family life with the child as the center. Rarely could one find heightened anxiety levels, and the problems that did appear were always worked out with a smile. In the *Donna Reed Show* of the same decade, life was lived according to a wish-fulfillment fantasy model in which everyone was happy and behaved as expected (how one should act). If sickness made an appearance, it was not severe or critical, and marital strife was not an issue.

Children growing up in suburbia in the 1950s were not exposed to fierce poverty, racial tensions, drug abuse, and street crime, although problems such as alcoholism and sexual abuse plagued society in secret. As a child, the 1958 Miss America was repeatedly abused sexually by her father, but she was only able to face and expose her tragedy as an adult (Coontz, 1992).

Family Behavior Patterns

From the 1950s and 1960s television explosion and its role models, the baby boomers and their parents got the blueprint for how families should behave. The priorities of the ideal family included primacy of the family, the woman's role as homemaker, man's role as breadwinner, financial mobility, the importance of appearances and hiding one's emotions. The repression of emotions during this time fostered intense feelings and values that produced young people with sharp eyes for hypocrisy. Many of the so-called rebels of the 1960s were simply acting out what their parents felt but to which they could not own up. This explosion by teenagers was a tacit agreement between the generations that children could do what their parents could only fantasize about. Teenagers rebelled against the stuffiness, falseness, plasticity, emotional deadness, and repression of the 1950s and early 1960s. Their actions were extreme, but they became the norm for society.

The baby boomers were key in exposing the falsity and unreality of the so-called perfect family. The media contributed greatly by assisting teenagers in exposing these misconceptions, that is, in coverage of their rebellious acts (e.g., bra burning or college uprisings) and their use of drugs (e.g., during Woodstock). The emergence of the youth market in the media planted the seeds for the destruction of the rigid beliefs of 1950s families and conditioned the young baby boomers to buy advertised products. Self-expression became a valued commodity for the "boomers" as parents looked on simultaneously in awe and horror, denying what was being placed in front of their eyes by the TV media and refusing to accept and take responsibility for the actions of their offspring. Parents may have talked about how things were freer and different for their children with a little smile of acceptance and relief but when asked their opinion about their children's behavior, they would express outrage.

Violence

Domestic violence occurred within families of all classes, but these problems were often overlooked by society. Coontz (1992) reported that between 1939 and 1969, not one article on family violence was published. Wife beating was not considered a crime. A well-known psychiatrist (unnamed) of the 1950s regarded battered women as masochists who provoked their husbands into beating them (Coontz, 1992). The psychology of the middle class was to build a new future and deny existing problems. The baby boomers, as discussed, refused to promote and maintain this national delusion, and the effects of their rebellion are still felt. The 1980s and 1990s talk shows were and are largely their productions. Although many today often go too far, they do allow people to express problems that might never be addressed. This is not an appropriate forum for real help, but it does bring into one's awareness the problems that exist in society across races and financial classifications.

Race

After World War II, American society became increasingly diverse. More Mexican immigrants entered the United States in the two decades after World War II than in the previous century (Coontz, 1992). Before the war, most Blacks and Mexican Americans lived in rural areas. By 1960, the majority of Blacks resided in the North, and 80% of them lived in big cities. This diversity was not reflected on television in the 1950s. The Hispanic gardener on *Father Knows Best* was renamed Frank Smith. During the late 1960s, however, television executives began to change their Whites-only mentality.

In 1965, Bill Cosby, starring in *I Spy*, became the first Black man to costar in a dramatic series, and he did not play a butler or a servant. By 1968, of the 56 nighttime dramatic shows, 21 had at least one regular Black performer. Blacks starred in shows such as *Julia* and *Sanford and Son*, about a father–son relationship. In the 1970s, *Good Times* featured a poor Black family and dealt with such issues as alcoholism, gang violence, busing, menopause, and Black-on-Black crime in a genuine and heartfelt manner. *The Jeffersons*, the longest running Black sitcom to date, revolved around George Jefferson, a bigoted, loudmouthed bully who barked at his wife and maid, despised his neighbors, and strutted about like a peacock. A Black Archie Bunker, the program showed that all character types come in all colors. On the other hand, the *Cosby Show* was about a Black family living in a New York brownstone, in which the parents were loving, nurturing yet strict, and committed to their careers and their family. Critics claimed this was an atypical Black family, but it provided positive role models for Black people.

The many Black shows of the 1990s depict life more realistically in terms of presenting all socioeconomic levels. What is needed today, however, are shows that reflect the cultural diversity of present-day America. A recent program, *American Girl*, featured a young Asian woman, but it remained on the air for only a short time. It is my belief that we need to see programs about different races living together in a peaceful and harmonious manner.

Changes in the Family

Traditionalists see the family as collapsing, whereas so-called modern thinkers see the family as becoming diversified. Modern thinkers reject the old stereotypes and create families with new structures. Their objectives include seeing families as self-actualizing wherein divorce is seen as a growth experience (Nadelson & Polonsky, 1984), finding ways to live in single-parent and blended families (Vischer & Vischer, 1979), and dealing with aggression and pain by expressing instead of denying individual and group rights. The makeup of the modern family has changed radically, with half of marriages ending in divorce. There are a multitude of over-stressed parents, single parents, fatherless children, and children who are home alone while their parents work. The working couple is the norm, no longer the exception, and this creates a great deal of stress and new problems for the 1990s family. Modern-day television reflects these trends; it attempts to depict families as they really are, in all their varied forms. To see that this is so, we need only to take a trip to "sitcomland," starting in Donna Reed and Beaver Cleaver's neighborhood, follow the detour to Roseanne's block, and then cross over to the other part of town and make a stop at Murphy Brown's, and we've gone from America's dream of an ideal to the real.

New Directions

Lessening Aggression and Violence in the TV Media

Today, the viewing public is exposed to a high level of aggression and violence on television, which encourages destructive thoughts and actions in our young (Primavera, Herron, & Savier, 1996). Although children's cartoon shows often end with a moral, the first 29 minutes are remarkably violent. The ever-popular police shows are becoming more and more graphic in their depiction of violence. Such programming provides negative models for people with weak impulse control and poorly developed egos. The popularity of sensationalist talk shows, however, strongly suggests society's hunger for a way to solve their problems. The television industry has a considerable responsibility to society. The themes and content of many shows should be reassessed in the light of their potential effects on the viewing public. In addition, the media should address the psychological needs of viewers and participants on talk shows and while trying to achieve high ratings should strive to produce shows that help viewers better manage their lives.

The media can provide more realistic and nurturing role models for families and society as a whole. Many shows, such as *Oprah Winfrey* and *60 Minutes*, do attempt to live up to this ideal. These shows address such issues as drug addiction and conflict resolution. Oprah has made a serious attempt to provide positive information and entertainment, and she is highly respected for the quality of her programming. Another show that comes to mind is *Seventh Heaven*, which is about a reverend, his wife, and the reverend's children of different ethnic and racial backgrounds, some of whom are adopted. It deals with real everyday problems in a respectful and caring way, the type of show that the entire family can look forward to watching.

Psychologists as Consultants and Hosts to TV Media

Media psychologists could help the media deal with pertinent subject matter constructively without sacrificing financial gain. Such shows as ABC's *Good Morning America*, *NBC News*, and WPIX's *Montel Williams Show* have used psychologists to work behind the scenes as experts. Psychologists could consult with talk show hosts on how to manage their guests and audiences or could host their own shows. The media would profit from having well-trained media psychologists as hosts rather than laypeople. Psychologists already have their own radio shows (e.g., the *Joy Brown Show*), which are successful for both the radio stations and the listening audience. This would provide the public with information and new ways of dealing with problems.

It is essential that television commit to offering its audience functional ways of viewing life and relationships. Some recent programming has attempted to integrate psychological research and findings with informative entertainment. In John Stossel's "Marriages That Stay," various couples' problems were presented in a very respectful and realistic manner with the help of a psychologist. The show focused on how the couples attempted to work through their issues over time, a very realistic way of educating the public and offering information that can be applied to their own lives.

Many news shows invite the professional input of psychologists on family, nation, and world events. Public Broadcasting stations could produce shows that demonstrate the realities of life and how to problem solve, whether it be adult issues (e.g., marriage problems, managing the family, or alcoholism) or child-focused issues (e.g., dealing with divorce through the eyes of their peers or how to socialize appropriately). Like the weather or sports, there could be a 5- to 10-minute slot devoted to a psychologist-assisted marriage or family segment.

Good News

It is important to mention one particular effort to change the course of programming in a positive way. I would like to applaud the recent trend of reporting good news, which seems to have come as a result of complaints by viewers that news shows only report bad news. If only crime, disasters, and tragedies are reported, people come away with a very negative worldview and a feeling of hopelessness about the future. Channel 9 (New York) News should be commended for its nightly "good news" feature.

Psychology and the TV Media Working Together

A major goal of psychology is to help individuals learn how to deal with anger, problem solve, communicate more effectively, and promote individual and societal growth. Television has the potential to be a great tool for good as well as providing entertainment; there is no better way to reach the masses. It could help divert human aggressive impulses but currently does just the opposite. It can provide practical information and education, as on public television, but there is little on network television. To this end, psychologists, with their understanding of the human condition, and the media, with its power to reach people and choose and finance programming, are a natural combination.

References

Barnow, E. (1975). *Tube of plenty: The evolution of American television*. New York: Oxford University Press.

Coontz, S. (1992). *The way we never were*. New York: Basic Books.

Freud, S. (1959). The *'Uncanny'*. In Sigmund Freud Collected Papers (Vol. 4, pp. 368–407). New York: Basic Books. (Original work published in 1919).

Friedan, B. (1963). *The feminine mystique*. New York: Norton.

Groves, S. (1983). *Soaps*. Chicago: Contemporary Books.

Larson, M. (1996). Sex roles and soap operas: What adolescents learn about single motherhood. *Sex Roles, 35* (1, 2), 97–110.

Lichter, R., Lichter, L., & Rothman, S. (1994). *Prime time*. Washington, DC: Regnery.

Livingstone, S., & Liebes, T. (1995). Where have all the mothers gone? Soap opera's replaying of the oedipal story. *Critical Studies in Mass Communication 12*, 155–175.

Miller, D., & Nowak, M. (1975). *The fifties: The way we really were*. Garden City, NY: Doubleday.

Mumford, L. (1994). How things end: The problem of closure on daytime soap operas. *Quarterly Review of Film and Video, 15*, 57–74.

Nadelson, C., & Polonsky, D. (1984). *Marriage and divorce*. New York: Guilford Press.

Primavera, L., Herron, W., & Javier, R. (1996). The effects of viewing television violence on aggression. *International Journal of Instructional Media, 23*, 91–104.

Riley, G. (1987). *Inventing the clever woman*. Arlington Heights, IL: Harlan Davidson.

Sackett, S. (1993). *Prime time hits*. New York: Watson-Guptill.

Vischer, B., & Vischer, S. (1979). *Step-families: Myths and realities*. Secaucus, NJ: Citadel Press.

Warren C. (1987). *Madwives: Schizophrenic women in the 1950's*. New Brunswick, NJ: Rutgers University Press.

Whyte, W. (1956). *The organization man*. New York: Simon & Schuster.

From Stigmatization to Patronization: The Media's Distorted Portrayal of Physical Disability

Rochelle Balter

This chapter was developed from programs addressing the depiction of marginalized groups in the media sponsored by the Division of Media Psychology at the American Psychological Association's annual conventions in 1996 and 1997. One of the initiating premises of these presentations was a comparison of how the media portrayed individuals with disabilities before and after the passage of the Americans With Disabilities Act (ADA) of 1990. Symposium participants established that before 1990, portrayals were usually stereotypic. Although it might have been hoped that by 1992, there would be some appropriate changes, it was disappointing when many of the changes found were merely cosmetic. People with physical disabilities were depicted more frequently; however, almost exclusively in background and extra roles.

This chapter reflects on historical media presentations of people with physical disabilities and how the depictions have and have not changed since the passage of the ADA and

The author wishes to acknowledge the assistance of Barbara Brauer and Allen Sussman of Gallaudet University, Betsy Zaborowski of the National Federation of the Blind, and Paul Donnelly.

concludes with suggestions as to how to appropriately integrate depictions of people with physical disabilities.

The Role of the Media

One of the most powerful influences in attitude formation in the United States is the media. It is estimated that most Americans (99%) have access to a television and that the average child spends more time viewing television than attending school (Elliott & Byrd, 1982). The media, specifically television and film, thereby become the vehicle that our society uses to transmit cultural views, normative behavior, and social values. The media truly have become our society's cultural voice. It is the way in which we both receive and disseminate our view of the world. The ways in which difference are portrayed reflect dominant attitudes and prejudices. The marginalization of certain groups, often to the point of invisibility, makes a powerful statement as to the status of these minorities.

What would cause the media to transmit stereotypic rather than accurate information about the members of any group? How is a group viewed when it is reduced to invisibility? Why do group stereotypes continue to exist?

Media Use of Stereotypes

Most people play multiple roles in life. Some of these roles are influenced by gender, some by profession or employment, and others by beliefs such as religion and philosophy of life. People further identify themselves by their race, ethnicity, country of origin, or other unifying group characteristics. Often the roles that one plays in life lead to a group identification, which can provide a sense of security and belonging. One may be a psychologist who is female and Asian American and who practices Catholicism. This person may be married and have children. Therefore the individual noted would identify with married people rather than singles, females rather than males, Asian Americans, parents, Catholics, and psychologists. Members of these groups may be expected to share normative behaviors.

Attitudes that exclude dissimilar individuals can sometimes be labeled as *prejudice*. Fishbein (1996) has defined prejudice as "an unreasonable negative attitude towards others because of their membership in a particular group" (p. 5). Fishbein (1996) has cited Milner, who described prejudicial attitudes as

> irrational, unjust or intolerant dispositions towards other groups . . . often accompanied by stereotyping. This is the attribution of the supposed characteristics of the whole group to all its individual members. Stereotyping exaggerates the uniformity within a group and similarly exaggerates the differences between one's group and others. (p. 5)

It is obvious that stereotyping is used within groups to strengthen group cohesion and survival. If group visibility and strength of beliefs are central to power and homogeneity, groups that are marginalized and rarely seen (invisible) lack power, and membership in these groups is conceptualized as unfavorable and negative. The majority of people do not want to identify with or be identified with marginalized groups.

A number of groups in American society have, at different times in their existence, been stereotyped and marginalized by the media. Before the Civil Rights Act of 1964, ethnic minority individuals were often seen only in roles concerned with servitude. They were portrayed nearly exclusively as laborers, valets, and cooks. They were seen as unintelligent, lazy, and scheming and often as speaking a type of pigeon English associated with the Deep South. *Amos and Andy* depicted the stereotypical portrayal of ethnic minorities. Some of these stereotypes continued into the 1970s and 1980s with shows such as *The Jeffersons* and *The Red Foxx Show*, in which the stereotypes were preserved beneath a superficial veneer of ridicule. In the mid-1990s however, it became as acceptable for African Americans to have their own situation comedies as it was for Caucasians. It is possible that because there is no longer a dominant ethnicity, there is no need to stereotype ethnic groups with the exception of Native Americans, who are either not at all visible or are seen in an unrealistic manner.

Gay men and lesbians, other frequently marginalized minorities, have also been the objects of media stereotyping. As Gross (1991) observed,

> the mass media play a major role in social definition, and rarely a positive one. In the absence of adequate information in their immediate environment, most people, gay or straight, have little choice other than to accept the narrow and negative stereotypes as being representative of gay people. . . . Typically media characterizations use popular stereotypes as a code. (p. 27)

Stereotypes save the audience the trouble of thinking.

The association between gay males and the AIDS crisis in the 1980s led to a breakthrough in the career options depicted as typical of gay males. The portrayal of gay men in movie roles advanced from mincing decorators such as Bronson Pinchot's role in *Father of the Bride* and transvestites like Albin in *La Cage aux Folles* (Murray, 1996; Russo, 1987) to terminally ill attorneys as in *An Early Frost* and *Philadelphia*. Whereas these films featured somewhat sympathetic portrayals of gay protagonists, the sympathy was elicited in terms of their illness. Their deaths made it possible for the audiences to be sympathetic while still maintaining a "safe" distance from them. It is interesting, given the epidemiologic data, that films dealing with HIV and AIDS focus so exclusively on gay males rather than heterosexual intravenous drug users and their partners.

With the success of AZT and various combination drug therapies, the life span of people with AIDS has been prolonged, and AIDS-based films have all but disappeared. The flamboyant drag queen has emerged as the new gay icon, as featured in such films as *The Birdcage* and *Priscilla, Queen of the Desert*. These depictions, even when sympathetic, are so exotic and flamboyant that they are distanced from the daily experiences of most audience members and, indeed, most gay men and lesbians. When the popular media encompasses depictions of gay characters integrated into worlds recognizable to most audience members, as in *My Best Friend's Wedding*, *As Good as It Gets*, and *Spin City*, the characters identified as gay are unpartnered and distinctly asexual.

Lesbians in the media are truly invisible, particularly in mainstream films. Although characters who play the role of lesbians have appeared on *Roseanne*, their depiction was stereotypic. Lesbians on *Roseanne* were depicted through the filter of the lead character's fears and prejudices. Lesbians tended to be imagined by this character as predatory and distinctly "other."

The most significant advance in the portrayal of lesbians in the media may have been comic Ellen DeGeneres' "coming out." *Ellen* offered a broader and more balanced portrait of its central character. Ellen's "outing" led to a great deal of media coverage and controversy. However, her ratings continued to plummet after her courageous public statement, which led to the cancellation of her show (Carter, 1998; Flint, 1998; Gallagher, 1998).

Older people also are a marginalized, although not a true minority, population. They do, however, share some characteristics with other marginalized or minority groups. Many people fear aging, with its accompanying difficulties, such as a loss of physical prowess, cognitive deterioration, loss of power, and loss of skills. Older people are not seen as attractive. They therefore become invisible. Hilt (1992) has pointed out that when older people are visible, they are portrayed as helpless and dependent. They are rarely seen as vibrant or attractive. They no longer share the cultural values of beauty, fitness, health, ability, and independence central to our society. Most people do not want to think about aging. In this, older people parallel persons with physical disabilities. Although television's *Golden Girls* focused on three aging women and one elderly woman, some of the stereotypes prevailed. Sofia, the oldest woman, was an escapee from a nursing home, "Shady Pines," and return to that nursing home was used to terrorize her. She was portrayed as having poor manners and multiple maladies, especially aches and pains, and as being forgetful (Gerbner, 1997). She was also unpredictable and needed caretaking. Older people, especially women, are often seen by society and portrayed by the media as useless once their physical beauty is gone.

This chapter focuses on the manner in which people with physical disabilities are portrayed by the media. Although people with physical disabilities are not a cohesive group, they share the prejudicial attitudes and homogenization that other minority groups have experienced from the media.

Attitudes Toward Those With Physical Disabilities

It is widely acknowledged that throughout history, attitudes toward people with disabilities have been predominantly negative. Body image is among the factors that enforce continued negativity. We live in a society that values intact bodies and strong physiques and that equates these with intelligence, success, and ability. "Seeing a person with a physical disability creates a feeling of discomfort because of the incongruence between the expected 'normal' body and the actual perceived reality" (Livneh, 1982, p. 341). Being in contact with someone with a physical disability may reawaken fears that the nondisabled individual may have about developing a disability (Livneh, 1982).

Portrayal of Disability Before ADA: A Historical View

A number of researchers who have written about the portayal of disabilities in films and television (Elliott & Byrd, 1982; Johnson, 1991; Norden, 1994; Zola, 1985) have described some of the stereotypes the media uses in portraying disability. The recurring unrealistic depictions include that of the superhero, the sweet innocent, the sage, and the obsessive avenger. These depictions are characterized by recurring themes such as pity and fear, menace and loathing, and innocence, and wonderment with the superhero being the least common (Zola, 1985).

Leonard (cited in Elliott & Byrd, 1982) concluded that of all the roles of people with physical disabilities portrayed on television, 40% were children, none were elderly, most were unemployed, most came from the lower economic class, and half were victims of some sort of abuse. Television portrayed the person with a disability as passive and neutral, neither hero nor villain. Some however, as in film, were granted miraculous cures. In a study conducted by Donaldson (cited in Elliott & Byrd, 1982), in which he monitored television shows for a 3-week period, it was shown that less than .5% of the television viewed depicted individuals with a disability, yet the estimates given by Donaldson were that 15% to 20% of the population had a disability.

There have been a number of memorable roles that personify stereotypes of persons with physical disabilities. Among the more memorable portrayals are Ironsides, the disabled attorney who rode in a van with a team of investigators; Helen Keller, a deaf and blind mute whom Anne Sullivan "civilized"; and Sarah Norman, the deaf protagonist in *Children of a Lesser God*.

Disability-Specific Stereotypes

There are a variety of ways in which disabilities are stereotypically presented by the media, as previously mentioned. However, there are also a number of strong stereotypes that are disability specific. Some of these stereotypic presentations have a caricature-like quality. When one thinks of blindness or deafness, certain strong images may come to mind, and these may be associated with a particular role that one has seen on television or in film.

Stereotypic portrayals of blindness. There have been numerous roles on television, in film, and in theater in which the protagonists have been blind. The only commonality that these roles possess is their lack of realism. In terms of nobility, *The Miracle Worker* is probably one of the most well remembered works. It appeared first on Broadway as a drama and was then made into a full-length movie. In this script, an intolerable, ill-behaved Helen Keller was tamed by a teacher of people who were both blind and deaf: Annie Sullivan, whose vision also was impaired. Helen was presented as uncivilized, dirty, rooting like a farm animal, having no table manners and no means of communication. She was indulged by her parents, who did not want to be cruel. The script clearly indicated that only another person with a similar disability could reach Helen. Although her blindness and deafness were not miraculously cured, Helen was quickly tamed and went on to help others with similar difficulties. Stereotypes abound in this script. One of the heroines, Annie Sullivan, is saintlike; the other, Helen Keller, is less than human and possesses few human habits. Until tamed, she could not be viewed as anything approaching normal. This allows the audience to feel safe through difference. Because Helen is an innocent (Zola, 1985), she is allowed a miraculous outcome. The miraculous outcome pairs her permanently with her savior, Annie.

In *Butterflies Are Free*, another theater play adapted for film, the protagonist, Don Baker, was a blind man trying to live independently for the first time in his own apartment. His neighbor, Jill Tanner, accused him of watching her. She could not or would not believe that he was blind. She was portrayed as shallow, unconventional, and commitment phobic. She and Don became friends as Don struggled for his independence. The third major character in the film was Don's mother, Florence, who wrote a series of children's books about a young superhero she called "Little Donnie Dark," who was blind and who, she told Don, she used to inspire him to help him overcome his fears. Even though the script is humorous, and one of the more positive depictions of blindness, written from the protagonist's and not an ablist point of view, the comic twist given Don's coping skills evoked pity and shocked many. Blindness is often associated with innocence and fear.

A television stereotype that lasted a number of years was that of Mary on *Little House on the Prairie*. Mary's blindness was acquired during her adolescence. She was sent to a "special school" to learn skills and remained there to teach others. She fell in love with and married one of her teachers, who also was initially blind. Again, the message seems to be that the only ones who can help the population are members of the same group. Mary is an ideal example of the *sweet innocent* disability stereotype. The scripts that used Mary as a main character were often filled with overcoming adversity, being a superhero, or dealing with sadness, including the loss of her baby in a tragic fire. Toward the end of the series, Mary's husband, at the urging of his parents, underwent surgery and regained his sight. He then returned to school and became an attorney. Although Mary and he remained in love, it was obvious that they were no longer able to share their adversity and that the relationship was no longer as close. Fixing the person with the disability, as if he or she were broken, is another stereotype, but only those who are heroic or saintly are eligible for such a miraculous cure.

Although the aforementioned are stereotypic examples of the presentation of blindness, there are others that are more hurtful to people who are blind or visually impaired: *See No Evil*, a short-lived television comedy (Pierce, 1991), and *Mr. Magoo*, first a cartoon series and then a full-length feature film. These are discussed later in this chapter.

Stereotypic portrayals of deafness. People who are deaf or hard of hearing have their own culture and their own language. However, to the majority of the population, they are sometimes portrayed as "locked in" and unable to communicate. Because of the difference in modes of communication, those who are deaf have often been pictured as lacking intelligence. In earlier decades, those deaf who did not speak were often referred to as *deaf and dumb* or as *deaf mutes*. This terminology is not only inaccurate but also hurtful to those people who are deaf or hard-of-hearing. *Hearing impaired* is another term that some deaf people find an anathema. To them, it means that the whole person is impaired because she or he cannot hear. Hearing individuals would often shout at people who are deaf in hopes of being heard or would exaggerate their speech, assuming that lip-reading was a common skill.

Deafness is not often portrayed in the movies. *Children of a Lesser God,* which was first a stage play and then a screenplay, addressed the relationship between a hearing teacher in a deaf school and Sarah, the janitor, who was deaf and a graduate of the school. Sarah was portrayed as angry and imbalanced. The story is a bittersweet romance focusing on the clash between the hearing community and the deaf community in which the teacher claimed that he loved the deaf woman, yet once they were together, all he wanted to do was fix her. The movie ended with the audience wondering whether this relationship would survive or succumb to the pressures of her disability. Again, the person who is deaf is seen as broken and in need of repair.

Another historic portrayal was Jane Wyman in *Johnny Belinda.* Although Jane Wyman gave an award-winning dramatic performance, her portrayal of deafness was far from believable.

People who are hard-of-hearing are portrayed in more absurd and demeaning ways than people who are deaf. They are often portrayed as elderly and dotty . . . loudly asking for repetition of what was said and just as often confusing the message sent.

Stereotypic portrayals of orthopedic disabilities. Although this may not be the largest disability classification, it is usually the most visible. Those who use wheelchairs, canes, crutches, and walkers cannot hide these devices and "pass." The wheelchair by itself, apart from its occupant, may be a fear-inspiring object. Many individuals have temporarily used a wheelchair either in an emergency room or due to a temporary injury, and others know someone who has had to use one temporarily or can imagine having to do so.

Different stereotypes are associated with wheelchair use. One genre is the wounded superhero who came upon his injury honorably while in the service of his country. The

Vietnam War was the focus of attention in two such important attempts: *Coming Home* and *Born on the Fourth of July*
(Norden, 1994). The heroes of both films were wounded vet-
erans returning from combat with some unwanted souvenirs
and a great deal of anger. These are considered films of en-
lightenment because the protagonists are pictured as being
like everyone else, with the same needs, desires, and a lot of
anger. They do not represent the flatness and passivity often
associated with those who use wheelchairs.

The Other Side of the Mountain: The Jill Kinmont Story returns
us to the genre of the sweet innocent. The story presents Jill Kinmont, a young professional skier, who sustained
a spinal cord injury and who for the first time had to face
the idea that the world is not all that friendly a place. She
tried to impress friends and significant others with her rehabilitation accomplishments only to be met with pity, con-
descension, and abandonment. She linked up with someone
who loved and respected her, and he was killed in an accident. She fought the school authorities and won small vic-
tories with which she seemed content.

The most damaging script and screenplay to those with
spinal cord injury is *Whose Life Is It Anyway?* An artist was
paralyzed from the neck down as the result of a vehicular
accident. Once he determined the extent of his injuries and
realized that he could no longer do what he wanted to do in
the way he once did it, he petitioned for the right to end his
own life. The message that the viewer leaves with is "better
dead than disabled." This is a message that has pervaded
history and resulted in people distancing themselves from
those who use wheelchairs because they do not want to share
in that terrible fate.

One of television's more friendly portrayals of someone
who uses a wheelchair was *Ironside*. The protagonist, portrayed by Raymond Burr, seemed oblivious to his wheelchair
most of the time and went about solving crimes with a
trusted team of attractive cohorts, then brought his evidence
to court where, as an attorney, he fought for his wronged
clients. Ironside seemed to attract the hopeless, the poor, and

the sweet innocents. In a way, Ironside was the ultimate superhero.

There are many more examples of physical disabilities that could be included in this review, such as John Merrick in *The Elephant Man*, who although deformed by his particular illness, managed to win love and respect for his talents and his good heart . . . another sweet innocent. Dr Strangelove had multiple disabilities but, unlike John Merrick, was seen as the ultimate villain. His disabilities were most evident when he was portrayed as most evil (Norden, 1994).

Do Stereotypes of Disability Serve a Purpose?

Social psychology has shown that people tend to think in terms of groups and categories. As was discussed in the introduction to this chapter, group cohesion is important to group survival. Each member of society, at different times in her or his life, will belong to a multiplicity of groups, depending on gender, race, religion, generation, profession, avocation, and interests. People tend to identify with those who share similar characteristics and often tend to exclude those who are very different. Different groups will eschew different value systems, some syntonic with their major culture, others not. Milner's (cited in Fishbein, 1996) definition of stereotypes stresses the attribution of group characteristics to all its members and the exaggeration of uniformity within groups paralleled by the exaggeration of difference between groups. Group survival is dependent on group cohesion.

A number of authors have written about stereotyping in conjunction with research on attitudes toward those with physical disabilities. Siller (1973) used terms such as *marginalization, inferior status,* and *minority group membership* when discussing how those with physical disabilities were viewed. Dembo, Levitan, and Wright (1956), and Wright (1983) examined the social psychological context of attitudes toward those with physical disabilities and arrived at a theoretical view often referred to as the *insider–outsider* theory, which they based on the supposition that most people feared developing a physical disability. It is known that the values of the majority American culture are beauty, physical prowess, and intact and attractive physiques (Goffman, 1963; Wright, 1983). When one thinks of someone with a physical disability, what first comes to mind is often someone who not only uses a wheelchair but also is dependent on others for all services. The assumption, Special Olympics aside, is that the person with a physical disability cannot engage in the activities valued by the majority society.

Those with disabilities are often seen as being of lower-class status, asexual, having a high unemployment rate, having limited intelligence, and incapable of running a household, parenting, or being regularly employed. Dembo et al.'s (1956) approach to disability is characterized by difference rather than similarity. The outsiders (nondisabled) protect themselves from the fear of becoming disabled by looking for and focusing on the differences between themselves and those with physical disabilities (Balter, 1997). If the differences can be made great enough, distance can be created, and fear of becoming disabled is reduced. Wright (1983) conceptualized a different yet equally rejecting way of viewing those with physical disabilities. In this theory, those with disabilities are seen as having superior powers, and the outsiders (nondisabled) view those with disabilities with admiration. In some ways, this approach is as damning to those with disabilities as the theory presented in 1956 because the person with a disability is never seen as a colleague or an equal. If the person performs "normally" he or she is performing at an inferior level based on expectations. If the performance is superior, then one cannot identify with that individual because he or she is too special.

The literature is full of examples of the depiction of physical disability and attitudes toward those with physical disabilities that are not specifically media related. However, one interesting study (Adler, Wright, & Ulicny, 1991) deals indirectly with this topic. In this study, two types of presentations were used in a fundraising paradigm, one in which the person with a disability (in this instance, a brain injury and orthopedic problem without wheelchair use) is seen with two different scripts, one emphasizing problems and need and written with a negative or succumbing spin and the other written in a more positive voice and coping style. The independent variables were the amount of money the participants would donate to the fictional charity and scores on an attitude scale. The results indicated that there was no significant difference in the amount of money that would be donated. There were, however, significant differences in the participants' attitudes toward disabilities. Those who viewed the coping condition demonstrated more positive attitudes toward those with disabilities than those who viewed the succumbing condition.

The consequences of stereotyping. When dealing with stereotypes of those with physical disabilities, one of the most damning factors is invisibility. Marginalization and invisibility serve to isolate people with physical disabilities and further stigmatize this group. Studies performed on the prevalence of the portrayal of physical disabilities in film (Byrd & Elliott, 1985, 1988; Byrd & Pipes, 1981) have found that a very small percentage of the films issued contain depictions of disability. Of the depictions of disability that are present, most are of psychiatric disability, not physical disability. The statistics cited for physical disability also include physical illnesses. The experimenters based their research on the *Monthly Film Bulletin*, which gives extensive production information, plot, and character descriptions, as well as a film critic's review. Even though the *Monthly Film Bulletin* reviews European as well as American films, the research was limited to those produced in the United States. The prevalence of physical disability presented was minor relative to the occurrence of physical disability in the general population. The results indicated that people with physical disabilities are often ignored, as they are in society.

Content analyses also have been performed on televised presentations of disability. Warzak, Majors, Hansell, and Allan (1988) examined 374 televised segments of 30 minutes each, which were randomly distributed across three major networks and three time periods, each in blocks of 3 hours. The investigators looked for the presence of disability, its relevance to the plot, and its valence in terms of being positive, negative, or neutral. The investigation was limited to "the observation of orthotic or prosthetic devices commonly used for support, balance" (p. 106). These devices included walkers, wheelchairs, crutches, canes, and braces. The observers used a training manual and also watched and discussed several hours of programming as part of their training to establish interrater reliability. The findings indicated that less than 1% of all of the intervals watched contained depictions of physical disability and less than 0.2% of the characters who were disabled had speaking roles. Most of the portrayals were neutral and irrelevant to the plot.

Marginalization and invisibility. When one considers that at any one time, 10% to 20% of the United States population has a physical disability (Dorge, 1995) and that less than 1% of the portrayals on television involve a visible disability, it seems reasonable to conclude that people with physical disabilities are, indeed, a marginalized group who are expected to be invisible.

The invisibility of people with physical disabilities has long been taken for granted. President Franklin Roosevelt was known to conspire with the press not to be photographed either in braces or in his wheelchair, as if doing so would somehow diminish the power of his actions (Gallagher, 1985). In previous eras, stories regarding sequestration of those with physical disabilities were common.

Some sociologists (Murphy, Scheer, Murphy, & Mack, 1988) have looked at the concept of liminality to explain why those with physical disabilities are marginalized. They argue that "the devaluation of the disabled seems to serve no economic purpose or political interest of great moment . . . it is . . . largely without rhyme or reason, but it is no less virulent" (p. 236). Murphy et al. (1988) describe those with disabilities as "victims without a cause" (p. 236). Liminal people, according to Murphy et al., are marginalized. They are between roles and therefore have no established identity. They are compared with those undergoing initiation rites who have left the roles of childhood but have not yet entered their new roles. Murphy et al. have described those who are liminal as "nonpersons making all interactions with them unpredictable and problematic. . . . The liminal are socially dangerous people and the solution is to sequester them, interacting with them only within the protective armor provided by ritual formalism" (p. 237). One of the signposts of liminality is invisibility. Murphy et al. have held out hope that those with disabilities, as others who are liminal, can establish a new role. Linton (1998) has pointed out that the terminology applied to the disabled and the term *disability* itself serve to create a distance and separation between those who are disabled and those who are not disabled.

Can Attitudes Be Legislated?

In 1990, Congress passed the Americans With Disabilities Act, which was signed with great fanfare by President Bush. This legislation is considered the Civil Rights Bill for those with disabilities. It mandates equal access in transportation, communications, employment, and public accommodations. Passage of the ADA and the attendant expectations raise two questions that bear directly on this discussion of the depiction of people with disabilities by the media: Has its enactment changed the way in which those with physical disabilities are portrayed by the media? Has it impacted how those with disabilities respond to these depictions?

It is interesting that soon after the passage of this act, more individuals using wheelchairs began appearing in television commercials for major chain retailers. They would be rated as neutral or irrelevant to the plot and were pretty much in the background. The same thing occurred on *Murphy Brown*, in which a secretary who used a wheelchair was often shown but never spoke or contributed to the action of the plot. Marlee Matlin made a commercial for hand lotion in which she signed that having beautiful hands was very important to her. A hearing person sat beside her and supposedly interpreted Marlee's signing, which was difficult to do since she never looked at Marlee's hands but only straight ahead.

Portrayals of Physical Disabilities After ADA

Has there been an increase in positive depictions of persons with physical disabilities in major roles since the passage of the ADA?

Portrayals of Deafness

Marlee Matlin played a deaf attorney in the television series *Reasonable Doubt*. The series, however, was short-lived but did show that someone who is deaf could be given a major role. Victor Galloway, another deaf actor, portrayed Meryl Streep's father (an almost cameo role) in *The River Wild*.

Heather Whitestone, a deaf beauty queen, was elected Miss America, and the controversy arose as to why she did not use American Sign Language. Rather than accepting her on her personal merits and appearance, as would be true of most Miss Americas, the audience became focused on her manner of communication. However, election of a deaf Miss America is a giant step forward.

Television also has begun to respond to the issue of deafness. On *ER*, an ongoing, award-winning medical drama, Dr. Benton's son is born deaf. The struggle that Dr. Benton goes through in deciding what type of life his son will lead and what kind of treatment or education his son will have are presented in both a realistic and sensitive manner.

Portrayals of Blindness

Interestingly, people who are blind were depicted soon after the passage of the ADA in commentator and color spots. One blind commentator who worked for *Good Morning America* performed and spoke about daredevil-type adventures that were obviously thought of as interesting because he was blind. This type of portrayal would not be objectionable in and of itself if more balanced portrayals were equally prevalent.

In prime time, it was another story. *Good and Evil*, a situation comedy about twin sisters in the cosmetics business, featured George, a psychiatrist who supposedly had become blind a year earlier. George's antics were the worst nightmare of a depiction of blindness. In the opening segment of the series, George went to search for the twin he was infatuated with in a laboratory. While there, he swung his cane, sending glassware crashing about him, talked to a coatrack about his feelings, and touched another male, believing him to be a female until he reached a point of recognition (Pierce, 1991), while the object of his affections cringed in a corner hoping to go unnoticed. The caricature was so damning that the National Federation of the Blind took action to have the show removed from the air. Pierce (1991) stated,

> the greatest fear that blind people and their friends had was that because of the public's inability to recognize the absurdity of George's behavior, the stereotypical clumsiness and obliviousness, to actual events around him which George exhibited would compound the problems blind people already have in employment and social interactions. (p. 627)

The National Federation of the Blind initiated a letter-writing and phone campaign and picketed network stations in various key cities where *Good and Evil* was being broadcast. The Federation also initiated a threatened boycott of products by the advertisers for *Good and Evil* to the point of picketing Unilever Corporation, a major sponsor of the show, and promising to stage a repeat of the Boston Tea Party in which they would dump Lipton Tea into New York Harbor (Pierce, 1991). Their efforts were not in vain. The sponsor threatened to pull its advertising, and the show was canceled. This result demonstrated that after the ADA, organized members of a disability-related organization had acquired the power to impact media portrayals.

The National Federation of the Blind had to contend with another stereotype in 1997 when Disney studios decided to reissue a nonanimated version of *Mr. Magoo*, to star Leslie Nielsen as the bumbling, nearsighted Magoo, who talked to walls and objects and walked onto swinging construction girders, yet corrected his errors as soon as he put on his glasses. The National Federation requested that the Disney Studios cancel their plans to revive this hideous stereotype with which many blind children had grown up. The message conveyed by *Mr. Magoo* was that when blind (or exceedingly nearsighted), Mr. Magoo is bumbling and incompetent; when he puts his glasses on, he is focused and effective (Pierce, 1997). The Federation scored a partial victory when the Disney Studios agreed to run a disclaimer at the end of the movie stating that *Mr. Magoo* was not meant to be a statement on people who are blind, nor their competence.

In *Scent of a Woman*, the protagonist went to New York with his sighted assistant and used his senses absurdly while he indulged in one last fling before his planned suicide. Although he eventually changed his mind about suicide, the picture of blindness that was conveyed was both unrealistic and negative.

The advertising world has made more headway. A recent television advertisement for Schwab Investments features a broker who is blind. The ad focuses on his abilities, not his disability. The only way that the viewer notices that he is blind is by the technology he is shown using, such as a braille reader.

Portrayals of Orthopedic Disabilities

People who have orthopedic disabilities or who use wheelchairs fare no better. In *Naked Gun 2 1/2: The Smell of Fear*, another Leslie Nielsen film, a wheelchair-using scientist and his evil double were played as comic villains. In *Hook*, the Steven Spielberg interpretation of *Peter Pan*, the depiction of Captain Hook led groups to protest the demonization of prosthetic devices inherent in Spielberg's portrait. *Forrest Gump* was a sweet innocent who magically ran out of his braces and dealt with his retardation; however, the real token of orthopedic disability in the movie was not Forrest, but his sergeant, whom Forrest saved in Vietnam and who, as a result, ended up with a double amputation. Forrest, the sweet innocent, saved this man again when they met, this time by encouraging him to join his shrimping business. The formerly embittered veteran, who had turned to drink, was himself magically transformed, became wealthy as a result of the fishing operation, began using prostheses, and got married. It is really amazing what sweet innocence can do. Is this a miracle, or a depiction of competence?

Television recently had one major role for someone who uses a wheelchair, but it was short-lived. *The Louie Anderson Show* featured Louie as a therapist. His wisecracking assistant used a wheelchair. It was a farcical role and not realistic. An ongoing role on a highly rated drama series is that of Carey on *ER*. She is an emergency medicine physician who uses a crutch. Carey's role appears to be a well-intentioned attempt to incorporate a physician with a physical disability into the script and still normalize the character. Carey's battles are always based on professional issues and not on disability. The attempt is praiseworthy and would have been even better if the actress had been taught how to appropriately use her crutch and if the role had been developed so that Carey had a social life rather than the character being unidimensional.

The news media has done a little better. John Hockenberry, a respected author and commentator, has appeared on numerous news shows and has demonstrated that a commentator who uses a wheelchair fits in well and can be taken seriously. Charles Krammenthaler, a columnist for the *Washington Post* and frequent media pundit, also a wheelchair user whose conservatism illustrates that physical disability knows no ideology, makes numerous television appearances and is highly regarded.

Where Do We Go From Here?

The prevalence of physical disabilities will increase as our society ages. It is now estimated that disability is a universal experience, that is, that everyone at some point in the life span will experience either a temporary or permanent disability that will limit one or more activities of daily living.

How do we go about normalizing disability and destigma-
tizing those with disabilities? How do we reduce the fear
associated with seeing someone who functions differently?

There are a number of steps that can be taken regarding
the media, especially in television and film portrayals of
physical disability.

1. The use of expert consultants who themselves have the
    disability that is being portrayed. This point cannot be
    stressed enough, that is, that someone who has a par-
    ticular physical disability can best assure the accurate
    portrayal of that disability. Life experience forces peo-
    ple with disabilities to learn ways of coping that would
    be foreign to even the best actor, actress, or writer who
    was nondisabled.

2. When possible, hire actors and actresses who have the
    disability being portrayed. Using Marlee Matlin to play
    someone who is deaf eliminates questions of authen-
    ticity that inevitably arise when the role is played by
    an actress who may not use sign language in her daily
    life. This reality factor can make such portrayals much
    more credible and help to avoid demeaning errors and
    the promulgation of negative stereotypes. The resulting
    greater visibility of performers with physical disabili-
    ties will also provide a generation of people with dis-
    abilities with appropriate role models and potentially
    reduce discriminatory attitudes in the general popula-
    tion.

3. As with any minority group, education of the majority
    culture is a necessary and ongoing function. When we
    discuss media, mostly television and film, we are dis-
    cussing a group of people, most of whom attend col-
    lege and many of whom attend graduate school either
    in film, television, or journalism. To ensure that people
    with physical disabilities are presented fairly and ap-
    propriately, it would be valuable to add a course or
    seminar to the curricula of these programs dealing with
    the portrayal of minority groups. One part of this
    course could then focus on how physical disability is
    often presently portrayed, the detrimental effects of this
    type of portrayal, and optimal ways of incorporating

physical disability into programming or scripting. This section would ideally be taught by faculty who themselves have physical disabilities. An added function of these courses would be to generate a literature that could be used for guidance by people working in the media field.

4. The use of members of disability advocacy groups such as the National Federation of the Blind to preview scripts or screen pilots, so that errors are not made that will result in harm to the image of any category of people with physical disabilities. The advocacy group could also be called on to act in an advisory capacity during the filming of a program or if scripting questions arise. Being proactive prevents a good deal of misunderstanding and may even result in increased programming quality.

5. Include disability studies courses in many college programs. If disabilities were demystified for the general population through interaction with people with physical disabilities, the general public would be less tolerant of stereotyping. People in the media, having learned that people with physical disabilities function and thrive and how they do so, would be less likely to incorporate stereotypic presentations in their programming.

6. Integration of people with physical disabilities in media positions. It is well known from previous studies concerning attitudes toward persons with physical disabilities that one of the most powerful ways to change attitudes is through interaction in a normal setting with competent persons with physical disabilities. Only through direct contact can stereotypes be effectively eliminated. This means hiring people who have physical disabilities with a wide range of capacities, in all areas of media including televison and film, to perform the full variety of production-related functions.

7. A few studies have been conducted that demonstrate the use of television and film on positive attitude change toward minority groups in children. As was previously stated, children spend more time watching television than they do attending school. One of the studies conducted (Westervelt & McKinney, 1980) dem-

onstrated that when fourth graders viewed a short film in which children in wheelchairs played with nondisabled children, the fourth graders evidenced a positive attitude change toward children who use wheelchairs. It would therefore be useful to have people with physical disabilities work with those who create children's programming to include portrayals of children with disabilities in both animated and nonanimated ongoing children's shows in a normalizing manner.

Summary

This chapter has examined the manner in which physical disability has historically been portrayed in both film and television. Despite the expectations raised by the passage of the ADA, people with physical disabilities remain a marginalized group who are rarely portrayed in a realistic manner or in a major role. Adopting the suggested steps could help to ameliorate this situation.

References

Adler, A., Wright, B., & Ulicny, G. (1991). Fundraising portrayals of people with disabilities: Donations and attitudes. *Rehabilitation Psychology, 36*, 231–240.

Americans With Disabilities Act of 1990, 42 U.S.C.A. § 12101 *et seq.* (West, 1993).

Balter, R. (1997). Using REBT with clients with disabilities. In J. Yankura & W. Dryden (Eds.), *Special applications of REBT* (pp. 69–100). New York: Springer.

Byrd, K., & Elliott, T. (1985). Feature films and disability: A descriptive study. *Rehabilitation Psychology, 30*, 47–51.

Byrd, K., & Elliott, T. (1988). Disability in full-length feature films: Frequency and quality of films over an 11-year span. *International Journal of Rehabilitation Research, 11*, 143–148.

Byrd, K., & Pipes, R. (1981). Feature films and disability. *Journal of Rehabilitation, 47*(1), 51–53, 80.

Carter, B. (1998, April 25). ABC is cancelling Ellen. *The New York Times*, pp. A20, B16.

Dembo, T., Levitan, G., & Wright, B. (1956). Adjustment to misfortune: A problem of social psychological rehabilitation. *Artificial Limbs, 3*, 4–62.

Dorge, C. (Ed.). (1995). *The statistical record of health and medicine.* New York: International Thomson.

Elliott, T., & Byrd, K. (1982). Media and disability. *Rehabilitation Literature, 43*, 348–355.

Fishbein, H. (1996). *Peer prejudice and discrimination: Evolutionary, cultural and developmental dynamics.* Boulder, CO: Westview Press.

Flint, J. (1998, May 8). As gay as it gets? Prime-time crusader Ellen DeGeneres led TV into a new era. But at what cost to her show—and to her? *Entertainment Weekly, 340*, 26.

Gallagher, H. (1985). *FDR's splendid deception.* New York: Dodd, Mead.

Gallagher, J. (1998, April 14). Ellen DeGeneres: "We're not coming back." *The Advocate*, p. 13.

Gerbner, G. (1997). Gender and age in prime time television. In S. Kirschner & D. Kirschner (Eds.), *Perspectives on psychology and the media* (pp. 69–94). Washington, DC: American Psychological Association.

Goffman, E. (1963). *Stigma: Notes on the management of spoiled identity.* Englewood Cliffs, NJ: Prentice Hall.

Gross, L. (1991). Out of the mainstream: Sexual minorities and the mass media. *Journal of Homosexuality, 21*(1–2), 19–46.

Hilt, M. (1992). Television news and elderly persons. *Psychological Reports, 71*, 123–126.

Johnson, M. (1991, May 6). Media miss the disability rights issue: "Courageous cripples" instead of access activists. *Extra*.

Linton, S. (1998). *Claiming disability.* New York: New York University Press.

Livneh, H. (1982). On the origins of negative attitudes toward people with disabilities. *Rehabilitation Literature, 43*, 338–347.

Murphy, R., Scheer, J., Murphy, Y., & Mack, R. (1988). Physical disability and social liminality: A study in the rituals of adversity. *Social Science Medicine, 26*(2), 235–242.

Murray, R. (1996). *Images in the dark: An encyclopedia of gay and lesbian film and video.* New York: Plume.

Norden, M. (1994). *The cinema of isolation: A history of physical disability in the movies.* New Brunswick, NJ: Rutgers University Press.

Pierce, B. (1991, December). No good for the blind in "Good and evil." *The Braille Monitor*, pp. 654–683.

Pierce, B. (1997, October). Let the old creep die. *The Braille Monitor*, pp. 616–627.

Russo, V. (1987). *The celluloid closet: Homosexuality in the movies.* New York: Harper Collins.

Siller, J. (1973). Psychosocial aspects of physical disability. In J. Meislin

(Ed.), *Rehabilitation medicine and psychiatry* (pp. 455–484). Springfield, IL: Charles C Thomas.

Warzak, W., Majors, C., Hansell, A., & Allan, T. (1988). An analysis of televised presentations of disability. *Rehabilitation Psychology, 33,* 106–112.

Westervelt, V., & McKinney, J. (1980). Effects of a film on non-handicapped children's attitudes toward handicapped children. *Exceptional Children, 46,* 294–296.

Wright, B. (1983). *Physical disability—A psychosocial approach.* Reading, MA: Addison-Wesley/Longmans.

Zola, I. (1985). Depictions of disability—Metaphor, message, and medium in the media: A research and political agenda. *The Social Science Journal, 22*(4), 5–17.

Tuning In to the Media: Youth, Violence, and Incivility

Lita Linzer Schwartz and
Rosalie Greenfield Matzkin

Small children are absorbing large quantities of violence that is likely to cause patterns of aggressive behavior, a comprehensive national study of TV violence shows. The research conducted by four universities over three years, suggests that much of the violence in cartoons is glamorized and sanitized, making it dangerously seductive to young children. (Stamper, 1998, p. A3)

The 1998 reports of television violence effects conducted by the University of California, Los Angeles (UCLA), in conjunction with several other universities, were headline news in newspapers across the country. These reports found that since the 1994–1995 season, "prime time . . . shows with violent content on the broadcast networks increased 14 percent, to 67 percent of all shows examined, . . . and shows on cable with violent content increased 10 percent, to 64 percent of shows. . . . *Nearly 75% of violent scenes on television, the study said, showed non remorse, criticism or penalty for the violence within the scene.* (italics added; Mifflin, 1998, p. A16)

The news in the real world was even more grim during 1997 to 1999 because of the dramatic rise in acts of violence and mayhem among juveniles. The fact is that homicides committed by juveniles have increased in recent years all over the world. However, in 1997, the Center for Disease Control and Prevention reported that "the United States had the highest rate of childhood homicide, suicide and firearms related deaths of any of the world's 26 richest nations" (Havemann, 1997, p. A2).

Here are some examples of recent acts of juvenile violence in the United States:

- In the small city of Pierre, SD (pop. 13,000), 11 young people, ages 13–23 years, 8 of them teenagers, committed suicide in a 3-year period, "about 13 times the national rate of 13 per 100,000 population per year" (Belluck, 1998, p. 1).
- On March 24, 1998, in a Jonesboro, AK, schoolyard, two boys, ages 11 and 13, respectively, killed four schoolgirls and a female teacher. This unexplainable murder aroused great negative reaction among legislators as well as the lay public.
- In May 1998, a 15-year-old boy in Springfield, OR, murdered his parents, then proceeded to school, where he shot and killed two students and injured others.
- On April 20, 1999, Columbine High School in Littleton, CO, was the scene of shootings and attempted bombings by a 17-year-old and an 18-year-old that resulted in their own deaths and the deaths of a teacher and 12 students.

Repeatedly it was asked why children need to have guns, even in hunting-oriented areas of the country. Attitudes toward guns differ so radically in various regions of America that meaningful dialogue about gun control is complicated and difficult. For some, putting guns in the hands of children is a carefully guarded rite of passage; for others, guns are weapons that only licensed adults should handle and only after completion of the most intensive computerized screening.

Graphic portrayals of explicit violence and brutal sexuality have exploded in recent years in virtually all aspects of our popular culture, particularly through the mass media. From television entertainment, to movies, to computer-generated games, and even to news broadcasting, juvenile as well as adult audiences are continually confronted by images of lurid behavior and killing. In fact, the sensationalization of crime and mayhem in the real world has become the mainstay of news and so-called docudrama. "If it bleeds, it leads" is the philosophy used by most local television news programmers to determine their evening lineup. In a media world in which competition drives sensationalism in news programming, virtually as soon as a crime is committed, news of it flashes around the world. This sometimes provokes copycat crimes in nature or technique. Indeed it would appear that for producers of entertainment and news, no act of violence appears too excessive. We hesitate to use the term *correlation* when studying the relationship between the amount of media violence children and youth encounter and the apparently increasing frequency of homicides by juveniles, yet there surely is a connection, even if it is not causative, between these two sets of numbers.

Statement of the Problem

We would suggest that there are two equally disturbing sets of issues evolving, both of which involve youth and the media. The first alleges that violence in the media, especially films and television, strongly contributes to juvenile homicide in certain circumstances. Many feel that there is an urgency to understand the media's role because of the continued rise in juvenile crime and violence. Others contend that the media are merely scapegoats being used to explain these crimes.

The second set of issues has been less carefully examined, although interest in this problem is growing as well. Recent research findings suggest incivility among young people is also on the rise and that young people are becoming more impassive, desensitized, indifferent, and/or cynical; less inclined to pay attention to politics, to vote in elections, to become involved in social reform; and, in general, more disengaged from the larger community. Researchers are trying to assess the relationship between this apparent disengagement and media content.

Our purpose is to examine some of the current perspectives on the interaction of media content (violence, sexuality, language, rudeness) and youth to establish whether these problems are getting appropriate attention. Going further, we seek to discover what positive impact the media can or does have on children and youth.

We must also be careful to acknowledge the positive role that mass media, news media, and the entertainment industries do provide for millions, indeed billions, of people throughout the world. Ideally, mass media have the potential to serve as a conduit for greater global awareness and intimacy that could ultimately contribute to better world understanding. That the mass media are major providers of information and entertainment seems almost an oxymoron.

We also wish to state that we do not support any form of government censorship of the media, nor do we have any particular political or religious agenda. There are times when people from vastly divergent political perspectives may share similar concerns and views. Certainly the concerns of many regarding the relationship between media violence and violent or antisocial behavior among children and youth cross and transcend party and political lines. For example, Senator Joseph I. Lieberman, a Connecticut Democrat, and William Bennett, a conservative Republican lobbyist and commentator, have both spoken out against dangerously offensive programming and have urged broadcasters voluntarily to drop blatantly offensive programs (Mifflin, 1998).

We have one overriding problem in presenting here: There is such a wealth of material, with so many dimensions on all sides, that only brief reference can be made to much of the data. However, we are including as many sources of data as possible.

Media and Youth

The Issues of Disengagement and Incivility

Descriptions of our youth as increasingly cynical, indifferent to the world around them, or "turned off" must be taken seriously (i.e., Hersch, 1998; Prothrow-Stith & Weissman, 1991). Student aggression and, concomitantly, disconnection from community are serious trends, according to a broad range of sources. Not only have surveys that chart attitudinal trends and modifications been describing problems of desensitization but parents and educators also have been warning about growing discourteousness; foul language; and cruelness on playgrounds, malls, and theaters, as well as at homes, during the past decade. Teachers' workshops, from as far back as 1989 in the state of Delaware, and as far away from there regionally as Los Angeles in the spring of 1997, have provided anecdotal material suggesting that children, even of preschool age, show a predisposition toward acts of aggression that does not reflect children's behavior of earlier times (see Schwartz & Matzkin, 1999). Even college faculty and administrators have expressed concern about a growing lack of civility among student populations. Two significant studies from 1990, conducted by People for the American Way and the *Times Mirror* Center of the People and Press, have characterized the generation of young adults age 18–26 years as plagued by an "apathy and alienation, in which the disengagement runs deeper . . . setting them apart from earlier generations" (Oreskes, 1990, p. D21).

A 1998 survey of 252,000 college freshmen from more than 460 colleges, conducted by the UCLA Higher Education Institute (1998), echoed these earlier educators' observations and concerns. This recent survey suggests growing numbers of students perceive higher education as a mere means to increasing their incomes and express far less interest or inclination in expanding their knowledge or their minds:

> As it has done throughout the 1990's, the number who said it is important to keep abreast of politics dropped,

with only 26.7 percent listing that as a priority. Political interest among freshmen reached a high in 1966, when 57.8 percent of students tuned in to current affairs. (Weiss, 1998, p. A3)

The study further revealed that student interest in social and environmental issues also has declined. Alexander W. Astin, founding director of the annual survey by the Institute at UCLA, described "this academic disengagement, and the continuing political disengagement" as "really troubling" (Weiss, 1998, p. A3). Although he did not blame the media alone for current collegians' attitudes, he did suspect that electronic technology and programming at least contributed to the problem: "People sitting in front of their screens playing video games, watching . . . is encouraging all of us to be independent, isolated individuals. That is going to lead naturally to disengagement" (Weiss, 1998, p. A3).

If adolescents are growing up choosing not to be involved in their communities, are turned off, and are not interested in voting, the causes for such attitudes must be sought. Although family, school, and religion are important institutions in a child's development, the increased role of the media in their lives must also be taken into account. How much of what and who children are, and what and who they stand for, is being shaped by frequent and prolonged media exposure?

Relevant Aspects of Child Development

The founder of the Television Project, based in Silver Spring, MD, wrote of her childhood in the days before television became an intimate member of the family:

> Without television, we greeted my father when he came home, we played together. I talked to my mother as she cooked dinner, my sisters created elaborate games requiring much cutting, pasting, sewing, and building. At dinner we sat at the table for extended periods of time

talking. We all read voraciously. With television, much of that activity ceased. (Pluhar, 1997, p. 64)

If one considers psychosocial development from Erikson's (1950) point of view, home is where infants begin to learn whether those in the environment can be trusted, whether they themselves are capable of independent action, how much they can question and explore, and how similar to or different from their peers they are in a variety of ways. The curiosity of the preschooler, and how free he or she is to exercise it, is of particular relevance to cognitive development as well. Stifled curiosity restricts the child's opportunities to learn, but this does not mean that the child should be able to explore everything anywhere at any age. It does mean that children should be free to ask questions and receive information and civil responses.

Years ago, before television, parents or older siblings accompanied youngsters to the movies and calmed them down when an on-screen image scared them, or did the same if they listened to a scary radio program (and there were many). Today, there is a question of how parents can help their young children cope with frightening media images, whether on television, videotape, or the movie screen. Today, young children are more often exposed to such images at home via the television screen and more often while watching alone. (Cantor & Wilson, 1988, reported, for example, that children indicated they would be less frightened and for shorter periods if a parent was with them while watching.)

The family—whether intact, single-parent, happy, or dysfunctional, small or large—is the child's first "school." Parents and older siblings, as well as nearby extended family, are models for the baby, shaping attitudes as well as walking styles, food preferences, self-esteem, and numerous other facets of the emerging person. Family stress and conflict, or the presence of a delinquent or criminal family member in the home, also are models, but these are risk factors that are related to violent crime by younger members of the family (Paschall, 1996).

Although family modeling makes the basic contribution to

child development, it is important to recognize the many ways in which media now intrude on the environment of the home and family. The uses of television as a babysitter are well known, a serious problem not only for infants but even more so for latchkey children. It is also true that media intrude in a child's life even *in utero*, as the mother reacts to images, including those that shock or frighten. Before infants and toddlers can differentiate between fantasy and reality, they may be exposed to discomfort and fear, to frightening images, and to high volume and threatening sounds that they perceive and react to but cannot understand. The incidental learning to which they are often inadvertently exposed can stimulate them in a variety of ways, including turning many, far too early, into carefully targeted consumers.

Other aspects of cognitive development include the ability to comprehend and evaluate what is perceived, whether through hearing, sight, or other senses; to conceive or perceive options or alternatives; and to anticipate consequences. Piaget, on the basis of *his* research, believed that children age 2 to 7 years could think only in one direction or about one dimension. He wrote that preadolescents could not develop options or anticipate consequences (Piaget 1954, 1963, 1970), yet even preschool children have certainly been observed doing such things, perhaps even verbalizing as they did so. A senior researcher on the study of television violence was quoted as saying that "children under age 7 lack the cognitive ability to consider punishments that occur later in the program and link them to the earlier crime . . . so in the short run, at least, they get the message that violence is condoned" (Mifflin, 1998, p. A16).

Schooling and child development. In today's media-fed world, young children who cannot yet read are entering nursery school and kindergarten carrying a variety of images drawn from their media experiences that go far beyond the peaceful world of Dick and Jane and their descendants. Even those very young children who may have been shielded at home from the most indelicate media images will encounter them after they interact with other young children. Whether they will pursue the most popular and generally scary images to be "in" with their peers or will be able to choose entertainment and tales that defy the most popular images depends on a host of factors.

One of the goals of schooling in most communities is to help the individual learn enough to be able to make informed choices and decisions. This is true at all grade levels and can be observed in practice even in nursery schools. Children learn in age-appropriate situations what options they have and what the consequences of their decisions are. The positive outcome of such training is to provide the juvenile (or adult) with the inner resources that encourage more socially desirable behavior.

Whereas schools try to provide support and assistance during catastrophic or emotionally traumatic events, it is most unlikely that similar efforts are made to uncover or undo the potential negative effects of media violence, real or fictional, on children. When a pupil at a school is badly injured or dies, many schools bring in mental health counselors to help the other students deal with the tragedy. In a time of war, tornado, assassination, a collective effort will be made on the part of the school to help youngsters understand what has happened, what if anything they can do to relieve the situation, and what is likely to be the long-term outcome. In our research, we sought to learn if there are actual school programs that teach children techniques of media literacy and critical thinking. We found that American schools vary in the degree to which children are exposed to and educated in the skills of critical thinking, although some citizens and parents would find independent thought by children a highly undesirable characteristic. Although there are educational materials and tools about critical thinking and media available, too few school systems have incorporated such media literacy guides into their own school curricula.

Peer Pressures. Peer acceptance begins to become important in children's early school years, when they compare their performance, their clothing, their size, and other aspects of themselves to those of their classmates. As they approach adolescence and seek their own identity (Erikson, 1950), however, youngsters also begin to pull away from the family nest, gravitating even more toward peer groups. Adolescents' self-esteem is frequently tied to how they perceive their peers perceiving them and is held rigorously even when it is erroneous. Acceptance by peers becomes of critical importance, and acceptance typically means conformity to peers' views and behaviors. Peers expect that all members of the group watch (and enjoy?) the same films, TV programs, video games and other activities, although the truth may be that as individuals they may not share these preferences.

One of the frustrations that caring parents face is that, even if they wish to protect their children from what they perceive to be harmful media entertainments, peer pressure can intervene. Once away from the parents, many influences can encourage media encounters that are not age appropriate. Children visit friends, go on sleepovers, engage with teenage babysitters, accompany older siblings to movie theaters, and are in general able to have encounters that go beyond what may be acceptable in the home. The emphasis on brute force or on cruel and demeaning humor that mocks the weak or ineffectual and the dominant anti-intellectual bias are pervasive characteristics of current American popular culture, which children almost cannot miss. Even during schoolyard conversation, children may feel pressured to know more about programming that may be inappropriate. *South Park*, for example, an animated adult series introduced in 1998, is considered to be off-color and controversial in its subject matter, going far beyond the limits of *The Simpsons* in language and story lines. Although it is intended for adults and seen at 10:00 p.m., 11- and 12-year-olds beg to be allowed to stay up and watch it. Younger children who may not be permitted to view *South Park* nevertheless hear a great deal about the show from older siblings, have passed on what they heard or saw to their peers, and have exposed others to the show's material although they have no way of understanding it entirely. During the spring of 1998, two other shows dealing with very young adults were introduced and scheduled in prime time. Both were characterized by a television critic as plunging the two networks to "new depths." The critic wrote that *Getting Personal* (Monday at 8:30 p.m., Fox) "is the most disgusting piece of sitcom dross to reach network air" and that *Push*, a drama (Monday at 8:00 p.m., ABC) "is a triple-threat: inane, inaccurate and often offensive. It is also maudlin, sophomoric, cliched, racist and homophobic" (Strauss, 1998, p. C6). Today's parents may find it more difficult to regulate their children's media viewing because the effects of peer pressure are so strong. The negative media portrayals of parental and authority figures may also discourage parents from taking controversial positions, because they fear they will be perceived like their media counterparts.

Incidental learning and unintended consequences. Most research recognizes that young viewers and game players will not be affected immediately by one day's worth of tasteless television or video games or even by several. Nor will the majority of children and youth be affected in the long term by one or two exposures to a violent movie or news broadcast. While high school and college students tend to watch fewer hours of television than their younger siblings (Signorielli, 1991, p. 48), there are many factors that can cause media impact on their attitudes, values, and beliefs. We must of course distinguish carefully between indirect and direct effects of media encounters. Two of the most important factors, particularly in influencing younger children (but teenagers as well), are cumulative exposure to violent programming and the lack of supervision by a responsible adult.

Incidental learning can occur when a television is on in the home and programming, not intended for the eyes or ears of children or youth, airs with no appropriate adults monitoring the experience. Such exposure to inappropriate material over time can provoke an overlay of emotional effects over time. Children who are heavy viewers and who seek out violent media shows can develop very negative impressions about the world, which can affect their interactions with others, including peers (see J. P. Murray, 1980; Schwartz & Matzkin, 1996; Signorielli, 1991). The example of children using inappropriate language because they are mimicking words or expressions they have heard on such shows, or who begin to ask questions about behaviors that they are simply too young to understand, is not an isolated and unusual situation; it has become a perplexing crisis in many homes.

During hundreds of hours of weekly broadcasting, advertisers and media producers create dramatic and arresting images that actually deny children/viewers the opportunity to exercise the critical thinking skills that families and schools are attempting to nurture. Indeed the frenetic pace of commercials, as well as "stories" on television, discourages reflection, thought, or analysis. Instead, the commercials, especially, appear to be intended to teach even the youngest children how to be consumers mainly concerned with buying goods.

Ideally, parents watch television with and supervise choice of programs and films when their children are preschoolers and on into the elementary school years. They can effectively ban offensive programs, but this has to be done early, not when children have become attached to those programs. Parents also can limit the amount of time that their children spend with television, videos, or computer games not only on school days but also on weekends and provide alternative activities for them (American Psychological Association, 1997). Of course, enforcing the time limits, if they are not at home, rests on the development of trust in the parent–child relationship or, if that is absent, some gadget that only permits the TV to be on at certain hours.

One question that may be asked about the numerous reports that children spend 3 to 4 hours a day watching TV: Are they watching, or does the TV serve as background noise? A number of reports suggest that children may watch one or two programs with interest but besides that the television provides "company" in an otherwise empty house (Freiberg, 1997; Steinberg, 1997).

Research raises more questions than it can begin to answer. How to protect the very young from exposures to seemingly menacing media images is confounding. What precisely *does* constitute "menacing media fare" to the very young? When should they have learned to associate certain kinds of sounds, pictures, and actions with what in some older children or adults is considered appropriately scary? With so many older children being left either improperly supervised or even unsupervised, the question needs to be asked: Under what conditions can television be "trusted" to serve as a safe and instructive babysitter?

The vulnerable versus the resilient. Why are some children apparently more predisposed to be influenced by large doses of violent media programming and/or to behave aggressively themselves? Todd Gitlin has been quoted as taking a middle position in the controversy about the effects of television on the individual: "TV affects different people differently and at different times. . . . It amplifies what's already in the works" (Seplow & Storm, 1997). This may be particularly true with respect to juveniles. Hardwick and Rowton-Lee (1996) similarly posited that witnessing violence live or on screen, especially when coupled with abuse and neglect, can contribute to a mental set that makes murder possible by youth in certain situations. Indeed, this combination echoes earlier findings with young male adults who had been convicted of violent criminal acts (Heath, Kruttschnitt, & Ward, 1986). On the more positive side, Martin Seligman (1992) looks at the whole individual and provides parents with clues to making their children more optimistic, ergo more resilient.

Vulnerable juveniles typically have fewer inner resources and relatively little adult guidance toward what is socially acceptable. In addition, they may be exposed to violence in their homes, schools, and neighborhoods, with few choices of activity other than to stay inside watching television or to join a peer group that may be wreaking violence. Those who are resilient, on the other hand, tend to have had caring parents who taught them how to make choices, perhaps even provided more choices, and taught them that there are consequences to behavior (Schwartz, 1991). They may also have discussed not only happenings during the day within the family but also what was seen on television. The parents have typically explained what was seen, if it was frightening or violent, and perhaps had the child act out a situation to increase comprehension and reduce anxiety (Cantor & Wilson, 1988). The resilient, as compared with the vulnerable, generally perceive themselves as having more options and of being able to weigh the cost of each option.

How Television Has Changed the Way We Live

Television has clearly changed the way we live— as individuals and as families. According to one sociologist, Charles Winick (1976), people have even been sleeping one hour less a night since the advent of television. In a week-long series on "How TV Redefined Our Lives," Seplow and Storm (1997, December 1) reported that "Americans spend more free time watching TV than they spend working out, reading, using the computer, working in the garden and going to church— combined" (p. 1).

In the early years of television, the family had only one television set, and family members shared their viewing encounters. TV programming had broad-based appeal (although there are critics today who perceive programming then as elitist) and was not so carefully marketed to specific demographic/consumer segments of the population as in this current era of cable and narrowcasting. The advent of television and its clones has changed the world, and these changes will not go away. Now, there are more families with three TV sets than those with just one. They are all connected to different storytellers (Seplow & Storm, 1997, November 30). In essence, this means that at various times within a single home, two, three, or more family members may be spending hours of family time alone in front of a television set. The issue of alone time for youngsters, whether in front of media programming or simply without human companionship, may need to be more thoroughly addressed.

Television's programming and images offer viewers the illusion of intimacy. In entering the private spaces of viewers' dens, living rooms, kitchens, and bedrooms, TV celebrities, sitcom characters, news anchors, and talk show hosts encourage the perception that their TV personas are who they actually are. Viewers, for example, trust their local television news readers. Such familiarity feeds viewers' desires for continuity and ritual, encouraging easy choices. Because television is so accessible and easy, people go out less and even visit others less. Because it is on in most homes for at least seven hours a day, it becomes more than simply a piece of electronic equipment or an entertainment machine. It is, in fact, for millions of homes in America, part of the daily and even hour-to-hour routine; a set of ever-present sounds and images that impinge on all other human and inanimate realities of the day and night. This white noise or background makes soundlessness feel empty for many who say they cannot cope with silence or with the thoughts and feelings they fear contacting. Life's routines become increasingly determined by TV time slots and commercials, sometimes at the expense of true human and/or family intimacy.

Media Criticism and Television Research

The mass media have been targets of criticism from diverse and often opposing organizations from their earliest beginnings. Motion pictures, for example, were condemned by professionals in the first decades of the century, who did not find motion pictures wholesome entertainment and who believed they would have a poor influence on children (Jowett, 1976, pp. 110–111; see also W. W. Charters on The Payne Fund Studies, 1933; Matzkin, 1985). The advent of television changed the focus of the controversy.

In its earliest days, criticism of television was muted, and in fact, there were many who received it with optimism. One notion was that the entire family could sit down in front of the TV set and watch together. Another widely held belief was that television had the potential to unify the country, producing popular culture that proffered a national cultural identity and educating us about our world (Carpenter & McLuhan, 1960).

But by the end of the 1950s, there were warning voices. In 1961, Newton Minow, then chairman of the Federal Communications Commission (FCC), observed that despite its enormous creative, intellectual, and information potential, he saw television as no more than a "vast wasteland." Thirty years later, Minow again spoke to the broadcast industry and observed that he was far more worried in 1991 than he had been in 1961. "In 1961 I worried that my children would not benefit much from television; today I worry that my grand-children will actually be harmed by it" (Minow & LaMay, 1995, p. 201).

Notions of television's indirect negative effects on children and youth are continually attacked by both television's cor-porate representatives and by the news media. In her Har-vard University public policy discussion paper, Sissela Bok (1994) identified and explored eight familiar claims the media industries continually make to justify their depictions of vi-olence in programming and movies. Among the most central of their claims that Bok reports and refutes are: "1. America has always been a violent nation and always will be. 2. Vi-olence is as American as cherry pie. 3. Television programs reflect existing violence in the real world. 4. Any public pol-icy to decrease TV violence constitutes censorship and rep-resents an intolerable interference with free speech" (p. 4). Bok rejects such rationales as simplistic, suggesting that the media industries refuse to understand that, like tobacco, as-bestos, and lead, television can pose serious risks to chil-dren's health and safety.

Problems of the Media and Role Modeling

Children learn a range of modeling behaviors from their fa-vorite characters on the screen and on television programs. From adolescent girls' efforts to invoke the "Valley Girl" in-tonations in their speech (perfected lately in movies such as *Clueless*) to the insistence on certain fashion looks spawned by entertainment and ads, we know that youngsters, en-couraged by media sponsors, are connecting with media im-ages. If they were not, the industry would not have spent over $500 million advertising to the very young in 1994 alone! (*Total TV*, 1996). It is not merely fashion images and speech patterns that capture the interest of viewers, including children and youth. It is attitudes, values, lifestyles, and behavior.

In earlier times, after great pressure from the public as well as special interest groups, the film industry adopted a Production Code that limited the screen's depictions of subjects considered particularly repellant, such as acts of brutality and cruelty to children or animals. The Production Code, also known as the Hays Code, operated from the early 1930s through the 1950s and even into the early 1960s. It censured the idealization of antisocial and criminal acts and criminal behaviors, monitored depictions of violence, and discouraged the idealization of attitudes, values, and beliefs perceived as anachronistic to certain mythic American ideals. All motion pictures had to receive an industry seal of approval to have access to commercial release in any mainstream American movie theatre. There were, in those days, crime movies, but closeups of the violence or use of guns were avoided, and criminals were usually punished. Although the Hays Code was at best problematic, controversial, and censorious, it made it possible to take children to the movies without endangering their emotional well-being because of violent content.

A similar code for comic books was adopted in the 1950s that banned "among other things torture, sadism and detailed description of criminal acts" (UCLA Television Violence Monitoring Report 1997 [UCLA Report], 1998, p. 1). The Hays Code died during the 1960s as the Hollywood movie studios began to use violence and more explicit sexuality to win back audiences from their powerful and growing competitor, the television industry. That code was replaced by a movies rating system that has been frequently updated. As television assumed a larger and larger role in the home, calls for restrictive codes arose from the 1950s on, although we would probably be amused today at what was considered highly violent then (e.g., *The Untouchables*).

One commentator claims that if you want to change juvenile behavior, you must change adult behavior, especially that of parents who are children's primary models (Males, 1997). There is much truth to this, as addicts' children are more likely to accept drugs or alcohol as part of their daily routine (though some may react by turning away 180 degrees) than are children of nonaddicts and children of spouse abusers are more likely to become spouse abusers themselves. The relationships between family role modeling, family/individual media selection and uses, and children's development need to be given more careful attention.

Mass Media/Television Content—An Overview of Major Formats

Data reported in late 1997 indicate that "North American children watch TV an average of four hours a day. This is more time than some children spend in class and *more time than many spend talking with a parent*" (italics added; Brown, 1997, p. SW6). A brief review of some of the genres of programming offered on commercial and cable television reminds us of how, in sufficient accumulation, these images can come to impact deeply on people's lives, values, and attitudes.

Children's programming, which consists largely of cartoons and animations during early weekday and Saturday mornings, has achieved high success marks because of the advertising it sells to its young consumer public. Much of the programming is actually packaged by advertisers. Some research suggests that children's comedic shows and cartoons, with their many acts of aggression and violence, are "teaching our kids to kill" (Prothrow-Stith & Weissman, 1991, pp. 30–36). Others argue that the "mainstreaming of violence" through media in general, but especially television, is at the least making violence an acceptable reality, and thus desensitizing children to it (Gerbner, Gross, Morgan, & Signorielli, 1980). PBS broadcasts for children are well known and loved and offer more imaginative and thoughtful efforts to encourage both entertainment and a love of learning. One new PBS series, however, a first for infants and toddlers, imported from BBC in 1998, has been quite controversial. Some critics of the show, *Teletubbies*, think that it promotes television viewing entirely too early in an infant's life and may even have negative impact on infant language development. "The Teletubbies converse in fairly accurate toddler-talk, often leaving out verbs, articles and pronouns, and communicating with looks and laughs and words that aren't quite right" (Lyall, 1998, p. 41).

However, in addition to children's media entertainment, the subject matter, forums, and formats of televison's adult programming have to be factored into children's experiential worlds. Television's more significant daily lineup follows a rigid routine that many viewers follow as closely as they do other routines in their lives. Programming, carefully researched by marketing and psychology researchers, is targeted at specific buying audiences who are expected to provide the proper (i.e., sponsor-demanded) ratings. Daytime, early evening, prime time, and weekend programming are carefully distinguished by genre and format, to deliver these demographics known as "product" to advertisers. And everywhere they get the eyes and ears of children, who they are supposedly not targeting.

Daytime Programming

Anyone who has ever spent a day at home with the television on knows the general range of daytime programming. Early shows include headline news broadcasts, talk shows, suggestive soaps, news and entertainment tabloids, game shows, reruns of older movies, and sitcoms. Alternatives exist for people with cable, such as science and history shows, C-Span, shopping and cooking programs, and even golf. But these cable shows receive mostly very low ratings.

Soap operas and daytime tabloid talk shows, with their emphasis on the bizarre and the dysfunctional, are among the highest in daytime ratings. Talk shows featuring confessionals by the bizarrely married, abandoned wives, abused children, or women who love murderers frequently unveil "secrets" and "mysteries." Although seemingly above the level of very young children, these shows can prompt misunderstandings, inexpressible fears, and anxieties. Curiously, many of the most explicitly prurient of these shows are run at 3:00 and 4:00 p.m., just when children are returning home from school, and they are easy for children to access. In fact, the entire lineup of late afternoon programming is centered around seducing viewers who are providers and caregivers, generally female, and who are at home. Repeatedly, the trailers for these tabloids and "magazines" tease audiences to watch for upcoming thrills and shocking details that will be seen "after these messages."

Prime Time Programming

Corporate media programming executives work diligently to create programming schedules that will keep people from switching channels, especially during prime time. Regular evening broadcasts include the many suggestive sitcoms, action–adventures with "mature" themes, dramatic series, and magazine/tabloids. Research (Gerbner, 1996; Signorielli, 1991) indicates that the effects of prime time programming and the litany of violence and sex-laden local news broadcasts that live and die by their ratings can provoke in certain kinds of viewers a darker and meaner perception of the world. Prime time programming is promoted as family entertainment. Today's more sensationalistic programming, with its greater emphasis on sophisticated themes, may, however, be encouraging early pseudomaturation for youngsters permitted to stay up for the later shows such as *Seinfeld* (last seen late in the late 1997–1998 season), *Friends*, *ER*, or *NYPD Blue*. Children today try to dress, look, and act more grown up, without having developed the intellectual or emotional dimensions of adulthood. Warning codes for "parental guidance" or "violence" are generally ignored at that point.

Among the most popular television broadcasts are evening sitcoms. These mainly lighthearted weekly sagas about different families, or groups of characters who live or engage like a family, are interesting material for media analysis, raising many issues and questions. In comparison with the sterile, "white bread" family portraits of 1950s and 1960s television, today's sitcoms offer more realistic, diverse, and inclusive notions of family. On the other hand, in their efforts to woo younger consumers for their sponsors, many of these shows create obnoxious, incompetent, or silly parents and other adult "authority figures," thus suggesting in program after program that only the young have access to truth, goodness, and balance. Of course, there can be delightful and good-natured humor in all of this. And it would be unfortunate if self-righteous viewers were perturbed by occasional depictions of adults making fools of themselves, for humans, especially adults, can indeed behave ridiculously. For us to laugh at our own foibles is healthy and necessary. But one can wonder why it is that the most popular sitcoms, which are essentially about families, tend to offer so many merely demeaning portraits of family life? Sitcoms such as *Married with Children*, (now in reruns) and *The Simpsons*, may offer more candor than they did in the days of *Father Knows Best* and *The Brady Bunch*. They also offer, however, a potpourri of crude, unlovable, and unbelievable characters, including teenagers who laugh contemptuously, patronizingly, and even cruelly at their family foibles.

Youth-Oriented TV Series

As we have noted above, there is evidence that children learn behavior and model some of their fashions, values, and manners of speech on those of celebrity heroes or roles played by celebrity heroes on TV series, in the movies, and from magazines aimed at this age group. Among the most popular TV series for youth during the past several seasons has been a particular kind of sitcom with youthful characters in their teens, 20s, and/or 30s like *Seinfeld* and *Friends*, and dramatic series such as *Buffy, the Vampire Slayer*, *Melrose Place*, and *Ally McBeal*. Sitcom humor here is driven by ridicule and insensitive or callous behaviors, which the tone of such shows suggest should be rendered and interpreted sympathetically. Many situations in the dramatic series also demonstrate scorn or negative relating, although *Buffy* does appear to have developed a more thoughtful texture over the past seasons. However, with their strong irreverence for adult or au-

thority figures and for many mainstream values and attitudes, they seem to play down the struggle with everyday
problems real young people face growing up. Irreverence is
one issue. What such programs seem also to suggest is that
most people, including young people, have no time or interest in introspection or in confronting the inescapable realities
of human existence. These are issues that can be treated both
humorously or dramatically; entertainment and thoughtful-
ness are not mutually exclusive.

Today's teenagers may still be kids, but their lives reflect
far different realities than the TV kids of previous eras. In
Buffy, the Vampire Slayer, Buffy's parents are divorced. Buffy
works longer hours than most teenagers did in past generations. However, most teenagers we can think of do not have
part-time jobs like she does, slaying vampires.

> Television and the phenomenon of teen-agers are about
> the same age. Both were invented just before World War
> II and burst onto the scene shortly after. Both are devices
> to create markets and sell things. Televison is one way
> children learn how to be teenagers. These pre-teenagers
> are part of a demographic bulge that represents a lot of
> buying power, now and in a few years, when they be-
> come full-fledged teen-agers. Teenagers and preteen-
> agers today spend a significant amount of their families'
> money. They go to the supermarket to shop for their
> overworked parents. They pick out much of their cloth-
> ing. With their status as loyal viewers and consumers,
> young people are probably granted more status and re-
> spect on television than in any other arena of American
> life. (Hine, 1997, p. A1)

Misanthropy and violence seem to be two of the most au
courant motifs displayed in prime time. The emphasis on
violence in programming directed at youthful audiences is
probably as clear in *Walker, Texas Ranger* as any other very
popular action program. *Walker* has caused the UCLA investigators "frequent concern" during the 3 years of their study
and has the researchers asking, "what are they learning from
it?" (UCLA Report, 1998, Ill.B.3). Walker usually seeks alter-

native resolutions to problems but ends up using abundant martial arts kicks and punches. The report asserts that this show has more violence than any other series on network television, although the show also frequently has prosocial and antiviolence themes. It seems worth asking a few questions about this youth trend in media: Is there any other reason for sponsors to be wooing teenage audiences than to gain new consumers for their products? Are the media unable to attract young viewers unless they offer up huge dollops of violence? How much time, effort, money, and advertising support have the media invested in alternative nonviolent youth-oriented programming?

Before leaving the subject of dramatic entertainment programming and violence, it is important to emphasize that acts of violence in and of themselves are not so much the point. It is the degree of dramatic expectancy, encouraged through the uses of specifically choreographed filmic elements, that manipulates and encourages certain kinds of audience responses. Such techniques as threatening music, slowed editing, silence, menacing sound effects, and long-duration shots that closely monitor acts of violence all work to provoke, encourage, and incite shocked or gleeful responses in viewers. Studies we have surveyed indicate that over time, excessive exposure to cruel and violent programming enures and desensitizes viewers and raises the ante for provoking positive response (see, e.g., Schwartz & Matzkin, 1996; UCLA Report, 1998).

Sports Programming

Sports programming is the single most profitable form of entertainment broadcasting (Biagi, 1998, p. 180); the cost of ads aired during sports programming is second only to prime time. A single 30-second spot on the Super Bowl is now beyond $1 million (Biagi, 1998, p. 229).

Events shown on television are probably the average person's greatest means of access to professional football, basketball, ice hockey, soccer, and baseball games, as well as wrestling and boxing matches. Sports events, both live and on electronic media, produce high ratings and are promoted as good family entertainment. It is probably true that in many households and at many ice hockey, football, and basketball games, families share their enthusiasm, especially for the home team. But sports entertainment, too, has its problems. Considerable physical violence between the athletes is expected in wrestling and boxing, although not usually the excess seen when one boxer bit off part of the ear of another. Still, as Young and Smith (1988–1989) have commented, "the media frequently convey the idea that violence is accepted, even desirable, behavior and that violence-doers are to be admired" (p. 302). When the player is rewarded or goes relatively unpunished, as happens in professional Canadian and United States' ice hockey games, for example, what model of sportsmanlike conduct is this for youth?

Examples of raucous incivility abound at sports events, where the behavior of live audiences is similarly sending the wrong message to young people. Cries of "Kill!," headlines on the sports pages that scream "War!," photographs of interpersonal aggression shown on the local television news, and stories that do not criticize players negatively for the penalty minutes they rack up or the yards they cost their teams by foul play (through flagrantly aggressive acts) are communicating an acceptance of violence to youth. The fact that many professional players are paid high six- and seven-figure salaries reinforces the message. Young and Smith (1988–1989) have concluded that "modeling studies indicate that young athletes learn how to perform assaultive acts by watching big-league models on television and subsequently enact what they have learned, especially in sports leagues where such conduct is rewarded" (p. 309). We would suggest that the effects of such modeling are not limited to young athletes.

On the other hand, even good parental supervision or TV rating systems may not protect children from offensive commercials shown during programs intended for watching by all ages, such as sports events. A case in point occurred on December 1, 1996 on the Fox Network, which was showing a figure-skating competition from 4:30 to 6:00 p.m. Eastern

Standard Time. An inappropriate commercial for a pornographic videotape available by telephone or mail, called "Cops Too Hot 2," was shown not once, but twice, during commercial breaks. Although it is clearly not illegal to air such a commercial, common sense alone would dictate that the hour and the program were not the appropriate venues for this commercial (Schwartz & Matzkin, 1999).

News Programming

Evening news shows actually may begin at 5:00 p.m. as dinner is being prepared and continue through the family dinner hour to 7:00 p.m. Children are often around the kitchen as the dinner hour approaches. As a result, in many homes, children from infancy through adolescence get an earful of local and national news that may be peppered with confusing, threatening, violent, and even frightening messages. Whether the parent present recognizes the possible impact of these on the child, or stops to explain what is heard or seen, is doubtful. For the parent, it may be just background noise.

Over the last several decades, it has become clear that *news* usually does not mean good news. Upbeat stories receive notice (a) only at the end of weeknight programming, (b) if there has been a major honor bestowed on a local celebrity, or (c) on Sunday night news shows when there is generally less hard news. For the most part, negative criticism of even local community leaders tends to outweigh positive comments on both local radio and television local programs. Since the 1970s, local news broadcasts have actually led the way in emphasizing graphic shots and images, as well as the details of brutal and catastrophic stories. To compete with newer news broadcasts and to increase ratings, they have adopted many of the accoutrements of entertainment programming, including images of body bags and bloody photos. The result has been not only a blurring of the lines between news and entertainment but also a continually escalating emphasis on sensationalism. A study of more than 100 news broadcasts on national, local, cable, and independent television stations during a 6-month period showed over half of the news reported had depicted some form of violence, suffering, and/or conflict (Johnson, 1996).

Some news stations, prickly over critics' accusations of sensationalism, insist that they are only giving the people what they want. One station in Orlando, FL, tried to reduce the number of crime stories it showed. The professional staff at the station and some people in the community applauded, but the station's ratings plummeted, negatively affecting its advertising budget (i.e., its income; Winerip, 1998).

Many television producers refuse to consider seriously the question of a 7-year-old's reactions to news at 5:00 p.m. or 6:00 p.m., when hearing (and seeing the evidence) of a fatal accident two blocks from his school. How much does a 5- or 7-year-old understand about death? Or the kidnapping of a schoolmate? Or the murder of a friend's parent or sibling? At this stage, few children understand the universality or irreversibility of death (Cuddy-Casey & Orvaschel, 1997).

It may take years to sort out exactly what the impact of the media feeding frenzy has been on children regarding President Clinton's alleged extramarital relationships. Just how much do children comprehend, and when? What does the child understand about the fuss and allegations about the president and a White House intern? He or she may know what a president is, and maybe who he is, but may need to ask, "mommy, what's an intern?" (Lewin, 1998). What is being communicated to children and youth when attention is so inflammatory toward issues of sex instead of issues of public policy?

Beyond the news and tabloid talks are the combative and often cruel political talk shows, broadcasts in which most children are not usually the slightest bit interested. Such shows as *Hard Ball*, *Crossfire*, and many of the Sunday morning news shows and political roundtables are as carefully scripted (Kurtz, 1996) as any sitcom. Using sound bites and speculating on political strategies rather than doing in-depth analysis of serious public policy issues like health insurance, taxes, or education, these extremely polarizing discussions take predictable "black or white," "up or down," "in or out" perspectives. Because such broadcasts are scripted to "beef up" controversies and ratings, they discourage respect for differences, or notions of compromise or amelioration among people who disagree.

For children and young people, who may not even be listening to these broadcasts but who live in an environment in which these "discussions" are background noise, the effects over time can be damaging; they can evoke feelings of malaise or anxiety or can heighten a desire for disengagement or further desensitization in those lacking the emotional resources to deal with such noise.

Gerbner (1996) believes that American television is providing a continuous atmosphere or environment that is harmful to our children and to the future of American democracy. Similarly, the American Psychological Association had as its newspaper cover story in March 1998 an article on the impact that information overload is having on all of us, young and adult alike (B. Murray, 1998).

Computers, Computer Games, and Chat Rooms

The makers of ultraviolent games boast about the dizzying heights of brutality they have achieved.

> Concerned parents and politicians argue about the need for standards in a world gone mad. But whatever the point of view, no one can deny that games are big business: Annual revenues now exceed $18 billion worldwide; in the United States alone, they total $10 billion, nearly double the amount Americans spend on going to the movies. And violent games are the most popular. (Ingall, 1998, p. 59)
>
> Violence in video games has become the target of widespread criticism because the games are marketed primarily to children (Hamilton, 1995, p. 181).

It is unclear from the studies of video and computer games whether the games arouse players to greater violence, desensitize them to violence, serve to defuse aggression, or do all three of these. Game designers claim that they attempt to steer children away from their most violent products by using rating symbols on the games (Ingall, 1998), yet they advertise the games in places where youths are bound to see the ads. They resist the idea that playing the games can influence youths toward violence. Some designers are quoted by Ingall as blaming mental illness on physical and chemical roots. Another asserts that if some behavior has to be modeled, aggressive behavior is the easiest to do. Role-playing games, generally quite violent, are also seen as agents of desensitization (Stetz, 1998). Two articles offered in two publications, one a computer magazine and one a city daily paper, left it unclear as to whether the reporters would permit their own children (if they have any) to play these games. Indeed, neither article offered enough information to assist readers in deciding whether they would allow their children to become involved with this form of recreation.

Just a few examples from one computer magazine will convey the flavor of these games:

- "Armored Fist 2": "fast, photo-realistic terrain with which to wage war."
- "Myth: The Fallen Lords": "In a world of walking dead soldiers, . . . Molotov-lobbing dwarves, and walking zombie bombs . . . truly unique real-time war sim."
- "Defiance": "Defeat and obliterate your enemies using Laser Lok targeting systems."
- "Pax Imperia": "The goal . . . is nothing short of total domination and the complete destruction of all enemy forces." (Boot Disc, 1998, pp. 12–13)

Such graphics as well as the explicit depictions of tortures that humans (or aliens from outer space) can inflict on each other also contribute to the idea that violence is the only way to solve disputes or problems. A very violent video game named "Postal" is considered one of the worst on the market. Apart from the insensitivity of the name,

"this is not a game about letter carriers being chased by dogs. The game refers to the term *go postal*, which some people use to mean lashing out violently, in reference to the sensationalized shootings at a few post offices in the United States." (Cook & Manning, 1997)

One interesting note in contrast concerns a game designer who is creating adventure video games aimed at girls age 8 to 12 years (Race, 1998). Her emphasis is on narrative and relationships, rather than mastery or power, although there are challenges to be met in the games.

Parents normally warn their young children about talking to or going with strangers but may not realize that they should remind their preteen and adolescent children of this caution as they become involved with chat rooms. Users typically adopt a "handle," or nickname, and can be as honest or not as they choose in what they reveal about themselves. Adolescents can be particularly vulnerable to the anonymity and acceptance they find on-line, sometimes resulting in live meetings that turn dangerous (Woodall, 1997). As is the case with other media, the individual potential for problems, such as low self-esteem, is usually present when this happens.

As we have underscored earlier, the impact of mass media on the individual child does not occur instantly after one viewing or one experience in a chat room or with a video game. The "magic bullet theory" to which social scientists in the 1920s, 1930s, and even 1940s subscribed, which suggested that children were merely passive receptacles for mass media messages, images, and impulses, long ago was repudiated. Nonetheless, we have learned that over time, children and adults can be influenced and their views shaped or modified by continual exposure to media messages.

A Word About Talk Radio

Talk radio offers a seemingly inexhaustible lineup of offending programming. From call-in complainant local sports talk, to the adolescent scatological humor of Howard Stern, to the insult-laden interviews of *Imus in the Morning*, to political comment and talk shows by ideologues like Rush Limbaugh and G. Gordon Liddy, the radio airwaves are full of strong and uncivil talk, some by hosts to call-in visitors. There are those who describe radio talk as "the electronic backyard" (Rehm, 1995). But people in the privacy of their backyards are not capable of attacking and cruelly gossip mongering to thousands and millions of listeners. Talk radio gets high ratings, which means sizable audiences. Youthful listeners, and young male adults in particular, seem to delight in its formatting, which continues to "push the envelope" in terms of language, political attacks, and rumoring, as far as is possible. What its long-term effects are on levels of incivility, suspiciousness, and cynicism need to be examined in depth. Its very popularity seems a persuasive argument for further study. Here again, we are not suggesting removal of this programming. Rather we are musing on its emotional attraction and its impact.

The Mass Media as Corporate Structures

Why is it important that the public have some insight into the structures and methods of operation of the mass media? It is important to understand that the television marketplace has become a severely distorting influence, in which competition and the bottom line have become the chief concerns of broadcasters and their sponsors.

Although American radio and television industries have always been commercial, for-profit businesses, which are clearly advertising driven, from the earliest beginnings of these industries, there were significant regulations put into place, which were intended to protect the nation's democratic institutions and constitutional and personal rights. The FCC was formed to ensure that no one media organization would be able to gain control of the airwaves, which rightfully belong to all of the people, and no one voice or corporate or political group would be able to control or manipulate the free flow of ideas. The FCC framed its regulations with the optimistic view that the media would serve as an enabler of freedom of expression.

Among the regulations devised to ensure electronic media's commitment to freedom of expression and to ensuring the public trust, the FCC required radio and television to maintain logs that proved they were regularly producing and reporting public service spots, community-oriented shows, and news, to have their licenses renewed (Biagi, 1998; Minow & LaMay, 1995). Other fairness laws involving American political parties' right to equal mass media access were also created. Somewhat later, the establishment of cable television was envisioned to enhance more local and public access to the mass communication processes.

Those media audience protections so carefully instituted earlier in the century have been persistently, if gradually, phased out over the last two decades. One dramatic 1980s broadcast policy shift, for example, was a new requirement that both children's and network news programming divisions become profit centers. That shift occurred when the longtime owners of the major networks, NBC, CBS, and ABC, began to sell their controlling interests to major conglomerates during the 1980s era of deregulation. Subsequently, the FCC has become so weakened, that fairness and community service are almost irrelevant (Auletta, 1991, pp. 193, 285). Observed Minow and LaMay (1995) of the changes brought on by the media buyouts,

> [they] transformed broadcasting virtually overnight from a public trust into one of the hottest businesses on Wall Street. In their celebration of the bottom line and their open contempt for traditional public-interest values, broadcasters began to restructure, dismantle, or simply abandon many of the features for which the public had admired them most—news divisions, children's programs, standards-and-practices departments. The number and volume of commercials increased, and broadcasters adopted an anything-goes programming policy. Children lack purchasing power and voting power, and the television marketplace and the political process have failed them. . . . That our children have been abandoned to strangers for so long, that the abuse every year becomes more aggressive and avaricious, is a direct consequence of our myopic new belief that commercial competition is the only measure of free speech and civic health. (p. 118)

Although Minow and LeMay (1995) are correct that children have been failed by the mass media, on the whole, it is not quite true that they lack purchasing power, because they have been given the tools to influence their parents' purchasing power very early in their lives.

Recommendations

Study Further the Attractions of Violent Entertainment

Why some children and adults are especially drawn to violence and mayhem and others less so, or not at all, is a question that deserves serious attention. What are the attractions for those who choose to engage with images of graphic violence, terror, brutality, and aggression? Are those who choose violent media programs more than merely different from those who avoid them? Do such preferences suggest emotional problems?

A recent set of studies, *Why We Watch: The Attractions of Violent Entertainment* (Goldstein, 1998), explores these and a wide array of related issues and questions from historical and other current perspectives. Their discussions suggest that family, gender, and psychological makeup do matter. Violence has been problematic as fact, theme, myth, and story since the beginning of history, the authors remind us, and in our time, no one is forced to watch any of it. Most audiences do not prefer violent entertainment, and most entertainment is not violent, they note. Nonetheless there has not been enough serious study of the specific attributes of violent entertainment and of the ways in which certain sensation seekers relate to them. In focusing mainly on effects of media violence, we may be missing some vitally important components.

Media Literacy: Teach Critical Thinking Skills

If children and youth are going to watch television without regard to adult preferences in the matter, then perhaps we need to find a way to harness this medium's attraction and protect their capacities for affect. Teaching children and youth the skills of how to use, discriminate, and enjoy the mass media, particularly television, should begin early in their primary education, perhaps as early as prekindergarten. Elementary school teachers might give assignments emphasizing critical thinking by having pupils describe details of what they had seen on a particular entertainment or news show and what about the story attracted or repelled them. Older pupils might be asked to compare the ways in which the print, radio, and television covered a particular news event, perhaps a local crime or trial, and to answer specific questions about the varied treatments.

The UCLA researchers have a set of criteria in evaluating programs that involve violence. Some of these might serve classroom teachers at various levels and in a variety of situations to guide them in their classroom discussions of the uses of media violence.

1. What time is the program shown?
2. Is an advisory used?
3. Is the violence integral to the story? Does it move the story along?
4. Are alternatives to violence considered?
5. Is the violence unprovoked or reactive?
6. How many scenes of violence are shown, and what percentage of the show do they constitute?
7. How long are the scenes of violence?
8. Is the violence glorified?
9. Who commits the act of violence?
10. Is the violence used as a hook to attract viewers?
11. What kinds of weapons are used? (UCLA Report, 1998)

Middle school and secondary school students could be assigned critical thinking projects, such as having to watch several selected program series for a period of several weeks or to watch several shows within a more limited time span, using these criteria as the basis for a report on the programs. Similar assignments could be made for films and for computer games. There are a number of new curricula evolving on how to address media literacy. The Center for Media Literacy in Los Angeles offers literature, tapes, and a variety of programs and support structures designed for differing situations, including schools, communities, and families who want to learn how to do such critical analysis and at the same time how to live with the media.

Model Conflict Resolution Rather Than Violence

It is our concern that there is not enough emphasis on exploring and encouraging the emotional development and well-being of children. We believe this involves helping children learn from very early on the values of respect, compassion, and empathy. We need to sensitize kids early, so that we don't have to worry about how to deal with desensitization later.

Across the country, psychologists, attorneys, and others are teaching youngsters alternative dispute resolution techniques. In fact, many schools have set up peer panels that use these techniques in trying to resolve differences among their classmates. The uses of conflict resolution could conceivably be the subject of dramatic or documentary programming, if only scriptwriters and producers could be interested.

Label Programs and Games for Violence as Well as Sex

In October 1993, Attorney General Janet Reno, testifying at a Senate committee hearing on television and violence, warned the television industry that it "had an obligation to reduce the amount of violent programming available to children" (Friedman, 1994, p. 775). After a few years of sparring and bargaining, the Telecommunications Act of 1996 and its companion, the Communications Decency Act, were enacted as attempts to assist parents in their selection of programs suitable for their children, to force broadcasters and networks to adopt ratings systems for much the same purpose, and to limit the access of minors to indecency on the Internet

(Schwartzman, 1997). "V-chip" technology, which permits parents to "lock-out" certain programs, was introduced in Congressional bills in both the 103rd and 104th Congresses (Deutsch, 1994; Spitzer, 1997) before becoming law. Specific aspects of the mandated rating programs have been phased in beginning in 1997, but attempts to limit exposure on-line have been less successful.

Part of the battle, other than the economic cost to various media powers, is whether the various restrictions are constitutional. To many, this aspect of the dispute recalled similar battles against comic books in the 1940s, films in the 1940s and 1950s, and violent pornography in the 1960s and 1970s, all of which were alleged to increase violent or lascivious behavior (Friedman, 1994). Interest in the legal questions is high if one is to judge by the publication of at least 42 law review articles in the period 1993–1997 that are focused on violence in America that may be related to media and questions of how to control it.

Encourage More Positive Programming and News Coverage

Public and professional (e.g., by Division 46) pressure on networks and advertisers to produce more positive programming and to increase the quantity of positive news reported may be helpful. Perhaps the Pulitzer Prize committee and the American Psychological Association might offer annual awards in this area to encourage such changes.

Expand Discussion and Public Debate About Issues of Parenting, Childhood, and Youth

We need greater public involvement, which might be encouraged through the use of electronic media and town meetings across the media channels and nation. It is vital to recognize that for our children and youth to grow and flourish, we must build bridges within our local communities and across our larger national community, so that we can decrease the polarization that has been evolving. All of us, as individuals, parents, teachers, business people, including those who are in the world of media, need to acknowledge more fully the interrelationship of human experiences from all dimensions and arenas. We cannot ignore the high cost that our consumer-first consumption-obsessed world has been creating. It is a world in which things or "stuff" you can buy, and the ability to consume them, are given more status than human feeling or compassion, or than humor, intelligence, or generosity.

Plans for public debate and discussion should include media analysis. It is essential that the public become more familiar with the complexities of corporate media and develop a clearer picture of how they are structured and of the economic realities that drive programming and publication. Many people, while dissatisfied with the media, wrestle with notions that the media are simply trying to do their job. The truth is far more complex. The greatest problem in doing media analysis, however, is that media themselves are not willing to publicize what may not serve their financial interests.

Modify Toys Made to Look Like Weapons

Although it is unlikely that a police officer would shoot at a four-year-old pointing a toy gun at her or him, this has happened with older children and adults. To avert such tragedies, there is a law that says that toy guns must carry a bright red plug to indicate they are not real guns (Goldstein, 1998, p. 3) Other weaponlike toys could be similarly marked and modified to distinguish them. It is unlikely that such modifications would be violations of the Second Amendment.

Summary and Conclusions

In her book, *A Tribe Apart*, Patricia Hersch (1998) describes in detail some of the highly unique notions of life that teenagers are struggling with in today's very public, media-hyped world, which cause them to feel isolated and deepen their experience of a generation gap.

> In the vacuum where traditional behavioral expectations for young people used to exist, in the silence of empty homes and neighborhoods, young people have built their own community. . . . The 1960's cemented in the public imagination the idea that treating teens as a tribe apart is right and proper. So now when teens act in ways we are not entirely comfortable with, we are not sure whether we should intercede or not. . . . In the nineties, the generation gap is a gaping hole that severs the continuity of generations. The new generation gap has nothing to do with social change, with intellectual questioning, or opposition to causes. Instead it arises from a new social reality. Today's kids have an abundance of that "space" the sixties kids coveted, enough to do their "own thing" with great regularity. Their dramatic separation from the adult world is rarely considered as a phenomenon in its own right, yet it may be the key to that life in the shadows. (pp. 20–23)

Youth's perspective today, according to their own words in Hersch's book, is far bleaker and less focused on engagement with community. How youth come to perceive the world occurs through a convergence of multiple realities: those of home and family, of neighborhood, of school, and of the other newer, technologically sophisticated media forces in the environment. The complex of messages and images that bombard youth daily interface with their moment-to-moment lived worlds. There is far more alone time for children and youth today and far more exposure to adult realities that they are not emotionally prepared to integrate. Although good parenting, which offers a sense of belonging, love, support, and nurturing, is of primary importance, other potentially darker influences can now impact more intensely than they used to, disrupting a child's sense of equilibrium and optimism. And if the family's life world is withholding, threatening, or simply indifferent, or if the youngster feels underappreciated or unrecognized, such threatening and unhappy images will have more resonance for her or him.

The responsibility for reducing homicide and stemming desensitization and disengagement from the community does not lie only with the media. It is the family's responsibility to protect children, to teach children how to think and make choices and to feel safe, from their early years, and how to be good members of the community as well as how to use nonviolent responses to deal with frustration and disagreement. Unfortunately, across this country, there are parents or families who are unable or unwilling to assume this responsibility. Then it becomes the community's responsibility to step in, because these lessons must be taught for the benefit and protection of everyone. Further, these positive approaches should be reinforced by the schools from the time children enter their care. As Marian Wright Edelman (1989), President of the Children's Defense Fund, wrote, "Preventive investment in children and families is neither a luxury nor a choice. It is a national necessity" (p. 18).

Finally, in the best of all possible situations, the principles of behavior modification ought to be applied to the media. When the media emphasize story content rather than gratuitous violence, they should be reinforced positively by the public. Conversely, when violence is overplayed, the media product should be shunned by the public.

We conclude that juvenile homicide and disengagement from family and community are serious products of the interaction of many things, several of which are familiar to psychologists: inadequate child-rearing, familial dysfunction, individual frustration, society's neglect, and inappropriate media content. Clearly there is a need for different segments of society to work together, and psychologists can work constructively with each of them. If we are going to demand a caring society, we must begin by being positive forces for the caring processes.

References

American Psychological Association. (1997, March 16). *Violence on television: What do children learn? What can parents do?* [On-Line]. Available: http://www.apa.org/pubinfo/violence.html

Auletta, K. (1991). *Three blind mice: How the TV networks lost their way.* New York: Random House.

Belluck, P. (1998, April 5). In little city safe from violence, rash of suicides leaves scars. *The New York Times,* pp. 1, 18.

Biagi, S. (1998). *Media impact* (3rd ed.). Belmont, CA: Wadsworth.

Bok, S. (1994, April). *TV violence, children and the press: Eight rationales inhibiting public policy debate* [Discussion paper]. Cambridge, MA: Harvard University, The Joan Shorenstein Center on the Press, Politics and Public Policy.

Boot Disc. (1998, February). *Boot,* pp. 12–13.

Brown, L. (1997, December 13). The tube that rocks the cradle. *The Toronto Star,* p. SW6.

Cantor, J., & Wilson, B. J. (1988). Helping children cope with frightening media presentations. *Current Psychology: Research and Reviews, 7,* 58–75.

Carpenter, E., & McLuhan, M. (Eds.). (1960). *Explorations in communication.* Beacon Hill, MA: Beacon Press.

Charters, W. W. (Ed.). (1933). *Motion pictures and youth: The Payne Fund Studies.* New York: Macmillan.

Cook, P., & Manning, S. (1997, October 30). Violence of postal game is alarmingly over the line. *The Philadelphia Inquirer,* pp. F1, F5.

Cuddy-Casey, M., & Orvaschel, H. (1997). Children's understanding of death in relation to child suicidality and homicidality. *Clinical Psychology Review, 17,* 33–45.

Deutsch, B. P. (1994). Wile E. Coyote, Acme explosives and the First Amendment: The unconstitutionality of regulating violence on broadcast television [Note]. *Brooklyn Law Review, 60,* 1101–1133.

Edelman, M. W. (1989). Invest in our young—Or else. *Human Rights, 16* (2), 18–21, 46.

Erikson, E. H. (1950). *Childhood and society.* New York: Norton.

Freiberg, P. (1997, September). Latchkey kids not always trouble-prone. *APA Monitor,* p. 48.

Friedman, L. (1994). Television and violence: A symposium dean's introductory remarks. *Hofstra Law Review, 22,* 773–779.

Gerbner, G. (1996). The stories we tell. *Media Development, 4,* 13–17.

Gerbner, G., Gross, L., Morgan, M., & Signorielli, N. (1980). The "mainstreaming" of America: Violence Profile No. 11. *Journal of Communication, 30* (3), 10–29.

Goldstein, J. H. (Ed.). (1998). *Why we watch: The attractions of violent entertainment*. New York: Oxford University Press.

Hamilton, M. (1995). Graphic violence in computer and video games: Is legislation the answer? *Dickinson Law Review, 100*, 181–209.

Hardwick, P. J., & Rowton-Lee, M. A. (1996). Adolescent homicide: Towards assessment of risk. *Journal of Adolescence, 19*, 263–276.

Havemann, J. (1997, February 7). U.S. tops survey on homicides of children: The United States also had the highest rate of childhood suicide. *The Philadelphia Inquirer*, p. A2.

Heath, L., Kruttschnitt, C., & Ward, D. (1986). Television and violent criminal behavior: Beyond the bobo doll. *Violence and Victim, 1*, 177–190.

Hersch, P. (1998). *A tribe apart: A journey into the heart of American adolescence*. New York: Fawcett Columbine.

Hine, T. (1997, October 26). TV's teen-agers: An insecure, world-weary lot. *The New York Times Sunday*, pp. A1, A38.

Ingall, M. (1998, February). Killer games: Violent CDs. Harmless fun or psycho prep schools? *Computer Life*, pp. 58–60, 75.

Johnson, R. N. (1996). Bad news revisited: The portrayal of violence, conflict, and suffering on television news. *Peace and Conflict: Journal of Peace Psychology, 2*, 201–216.

Jowett, G. (1976). *Film: The democratic art*. Boston: Little, Brown

Kurtz, H. (1996). *Hot air: All talk, all the time*. New York: Random House.

Lewin, T. (1998, February 1). The children: "Mommy, what's an intern?" And other hard topics. *The New York Times*, p. 20.

Lyall, S. (1998, January 11). Tubbies say, "Eh-oh." Parents say, "Uh-oh." *The New York Times*, sec. 2, p. 41.

Males, M. (1997, October). Who us? Stop blaming kids and TV for crime and substance abuse. *The Progressive, 61* (10), 25.

Matzkin, R. G. (1985). *The film encounter in the life-world of urban couples: A uses and gratifications study*. Unpublished doctoral dissertation, Columbia University, Teachers College, New York.

Mifflin, L. (1998, April 17). Increase seen in number of violent TV programs. *The New York Times*, p. A16.

Minow, N. N., & LaMay, C. L. (1995). *Abandoned in the wasteland: Children, television and the First Amendment*. New York: Hill & Wang.

Murray, B. (1998, March). Data smog: Newest culprit in brain drain. *APA Monitor, 29* (3), 1, 42.

Murray, J. P. (1980). *Television & youth: 25 years of research & controversy*. Washington, DC: The Boys Town Center for the Study of Youth Development.

Oreskes, M. (1990, June 28). Profiles of today's youth: They couldn't care less. *The New York Times*, pp. A1, D21.

Paschall, M. J. (1996). Relationships among family characteristics and violent behavior by Black and White male adolescents. *Journal of Youth and Adolescence, 25*, 177–197.

Piaget, J. (1954). *The construction of reality in the child* (M. Cook, Trans.). New York: Basic Books.

Piaget, J. (1963). *Origins of intelligence in children*. New York: Norton.

Piaget, J. (1970). Piaget's theory. In P. Mussen (Ed.), *Handbook of child psychology* (3rd ed.). New York: Wiley.

Pluhar, A. (1997, Winter). Just say no to television. *Vassar Quarterly*, p. 64.

Prothrow-Stith, D., & Weissman, M. (1991). *Deadly consequences: How violence is destroying our teenage population and a plan to begin solving the problem*. New York: HarperPerennial.

Race, T. (1998, March 5). Building girls cyber rooms of their own. *The New York Times*, p. G3.

Rehm, D. (1995). Talking over America's electronic backyard fence. In E. C. Pease & E. E. Dennis (Eds.), *Radio: The forgotten medium* (pp. 69–74). New Brunswick, NJ: Transaction.

Schwartz, L. L. (1991). Resisting the powers of religious cults. In W. A. Rhodes & W. K. Brown (Eds.), *Why some children succeed despite the odds* (pp. 159–170). New York: Praegar.

Schwartz, L. L., & Matzkin, R. G. (1996). Violence, viewing, and development. In H. V. Hall (Ed.), *Lethal violence 2000* (pp. 113–142). Kamuela, HI: Pacific Institute for the Study of Conflict and Aggression.

Schwartz, L. L., & Matzkin, R. G. (1999). Violence, viewing, and polarization. In H. V. Hall & L. C. Whitaker (Eds.), *Collective Violence 2000* (pp. 109–154). Boca Raton, FL: CRC Press.

Schwartzman, A. J. (1997, October 13). Broadcast and Internet coalitions took much different approaches in opposing laws to rate the content of their respective media and got much different results. *Legal Times*, p. S46.

Seligman, M. E. P. (1992). *Learned optimism*. New York: Pocket Books.

Seplow, S., & Storm, J. (1997, November 30–December 6). How TV redefined our lives [7-part series]. *The Philadelphia Inquirer*.

Signorielli, N. (1991). *A sourcebook on children and television*. New York: Greenwood Press.

Spitzer, M. L. (1997). An introduction to the law and economics of the V-chip. *Cardozo Arts and Entertainment Law Journal, 15*, 429.

Stamper, J. (1998, April 17). Study of TV violence sees added risk for young children. *The Philadelphia Inquirer*, p. A3.

Steinberg, J. (1997, March 13). Rechanneling a child's attention. *The New York Times*, pp. B1, B3.

Stetz, M. (1998, February 8). Role-playing games: Are they good or evil? *San Diego Union-Tribune*, pp. B1, B6.

Strauss, R. (1998, April 6). Fox & ABC debuts sink to new depths. *Philadelphia Inquirer*, p. C6.

Total TV. (1996, August-September). Horsham, PA: TVSM, Inc.

UCLA Television Violence Monitoring Report 1997. (1998). Available: http://www-ccp.sppsr.ucla.edu/1997-97.htm

Weiss, K. (1998, January 13). Political interest is ebbing among college freshmen, survey indicates. *The Philadelphia Inquirer*, p. A3.

Winerip, M. (1998, January 11). Looking for an 11 o'clock fix. *The New York Times Magazine*, 30–36, 38–40, 50, 54, 62–63.

Winick, C. (1976, August 7). Class lecture. Symposium: *Topics in communication*. New York: Columbia University, Teachers College.

Woodall, M. (1997, October 16). Warning: Chat rooms may pose a peril to teens' mental health. *The Philadelphia Inquirer*, pp. A1, A18.

Young, K., & Smith, M. D. (1988–1989). Mass media treatment of violence in sports and its effects. *Current Psychology: Research and Reviews, 7,* 298–311.

Index

About the Editor

Lita Linzer Schwartz, PhD, ABPP (Forensic), is a graduate of Vassar College (economics), Temple University (clinical psychology/special education), and Bryn Mawr College (education and child development). She is also a trained family mediator. Most of her teaching career was spent at Pennsylvania State University's Ogontz Campus (now Abington College), where she had full responsibility for the College of Education and taught courses relevant to education and children for prospective teachers as well as psychology, women's studies, and ethnic courses.

Because she recognizes the influence of multiple interrelated factors on individual development, she has studied and done research in a variety of associated fields, including gifted and creative students, gender differences, cultural diversity, forensic psychology, resilience and vulnerability to cults and violence, and family disorganization. Dr. Schwartz is author, co-author, or editor of 17 books, more than 60 journal articles, and 31 chapters. She has presented papers and workshops both in the United States and abroad.